Productive Struggle in the 6–12 Classroom

In today's world of being able to find answers at the click of a button, students need to learn how to grapple with complex concepts. But when is that struggle actually productive, and when is it just frustrating or discouraging? In this important book, bestselling author Barbara R. Blackburn shows how to help secondary students tackle hard topics in ways that will truly aid their learning.

You'll learn how productive struggle is connected to intrinsic motivation and how to scaffold instruction so you're not just throwing students into the deep end. You'll also find out how to pick the appropriate level of struggle and how to scaffold learning for students. Throughout, there are tons of practical charts, rubrics, and examples across subject areas, along with reflection questions to help you apply what you've learned. Bonus: Each chapter has a QR Code that takes you to related videos and additional tools.

With this highly practical guide, you'll be able to help students enjoy the fulfillment, confidence, and growth that comes with working through a challenging learning process.

Barbara R. Blackburn, a Top 30 Global Guru in Education, is the bestselling author of over 40 books and is a sought-after national and international consultant. She was an award-winning professor at Winthrop University and has taught early childhood, elementary, middle, and high school students.

Productive Struggle in the 6–12 Classroom

Strategies Across the Content Areas

Barbara R. Blackburn

Routledge
Taylor & Francis Group
NEW YORK AND LONDON

Designed cover image: Getty Images

First published 2026
by Routledge
605 Third Avenue, New York, NY 10158

and by Routledge
4 Park Square, Milton Park, Abingdon, Oxon, OX14 4RN

Routledge is an imprint of the Taylor & Francis Group, an informa business

© 2026 Barbara R. Blackburn

The right of Barbara R. Blackburn to be identified as author of this work has been asserted in accordance with sections 77 and 78 of the Copyright, Designs and Patents Act 1988.

All rights reserved. No part of this book may be reprinted or reproduced or utilised in any form or by any electronic, mechanical, or other means, now known or hereafter invented, including photocopying and recording, or in any information storage or retrieval system, without permission in writing from the publishers.

Trademark notice: Product or corporate names may be trademarks or registered trademarks, and are used only for identification and explanation without intent to infringe.

For Product Safety Concerns and Information please contact our EU representative GPSR@taylorandfrancis.com. Taylor & Francis Verlag GmbH, Kaufingerstraße 24, 80331 München, Germany.

ISBN: 978-1-041-19699-0 (hbk)
ISBN: 978-1-041-19697-6 (pbk)
ISBN: 978-1-003-71291-6 (ebk)

DOI: 10.4324/9781003712916

Typeset in Palatino
by Apex CoVantage, LLC

Access the Support Material: Routledge.com/9781041196976

Support Material

The following tools from the book are also available on our website as free downloads, so you can easily print and reproduce them for classroom use. To access the materials, go to the book product page at www.Routledge.com/9781041196976 and click on the link that says Support Material.

Frustration Anchor Chart

Anchor Chart Primary Source Documents

Rubric for Teacher Behaviors

Rubric for Student Behaviors

Chart for Determining if Text is Too Hard

Explanation vs Justification

Academic Conversations Expectations

How to Get Help

Toolbox Check

Peer Observations

I dedicate this book to Lauren Davis, my editor for over 15 years and now also my publisher. She encourages, coaches, and inspires, and helps me be the best writer I can be. She is more than my editor and publisher—she is my dear friend.

Contents

Acknowledgments xi
Meet the Author xiii

Introduction 1

1   The Basics of Productive Struggle 3

2   Student Motivation and Learning Dispositions 17

3   Instruction for Productive Struggle 43

4   What Is the Right Level for Productive Struggle? 87

5   Scaffolding for Productive Struggle 109

6   Assessment in the Productive Struggle Classroom 167

7   Common Concerns About Productive Struggle 199

8   Collaborating for Productive Struggle 213

    Bibliography 225

Acknowledgments

For my husband, Pete, who has the biggest heart of anyone I know.

For my mom, who, even with her Alzheimer's, always provides me a glimpse of hope!

For Darrin Parker, whose strength amazes me.

For Missy Miles, whose creativity as a teacher inspires me.

For Brad Witzel, who helped me refine my thoughts about the basis for productive struggle.

For the leaders and teachers at Freedom Middle School in Tennessee, I respect your commitment to growth—both your own and your students.

Dr. Katie Perez for her fabulous Productive Struggle chart.

Emma Capel continues to design outstanding covers for my books.

Autumn Spalding's support in production makes my books come to life.

For the teachers and leaders both here in the United States and around the world (shout out to Australia), I admire your love for your students and your dedication to help them learn.

Meet the Author

Barbara R. Blackburn

Ranked in the Top 30 Global Gurus in Education, Barbara has dedicated her life to raising the level of expectation and motivation for professional educators and students alike. What differentiates Barbara's approximately 40 books are her easily executable concrete examples based on decades of experience as a teacher, professor, and consultant. Barbara's dedication to education was inspired in her early years by her parents, Bob and Rose. Her father's doctorate and lifetime career as a professor taught her the importance of professional training. Her mother's career as school secretary shaped Barbara's appreciation of the effort all staff play in the education of every child.

Barbara has taught early childhood, elementary, middle, and high school students and has served as an educational consultant for three publishing companies. She holds a master's degree in school administration and was certified as both a teacher and a school principal in North Carolina. She received her PhD in curriculum and teaching from the University of North Carolina at Greensboro. In 2006, she received the award for Outstanding Junior Professor at Winthrop University. She left her position at the University of North Carolina at Charlotte to write and speak full-time.

In addition to speaking at state, national, and international conferences, she also regularly presents virtual and on-site workshops for teachers and administrators in elementary, middle, and high schools across the world. Her workshops are lively and engaging and filled with practical information. Topics include productive struggle, high expectations, scaffolding for support, instructional strategies, and leadership.

Introduction

I became intrigued by the notion of productive struggle several years ago. When I was a teacher, my students didn't want to do any work that required . . . well, work! They only wanted things that were easy. Over time, I was able to convince them that struggling to learn at higher levels was normal, and even positive. But it was a challenge, and some remained resistant. After I left my job as a teacher, I became an educational consultant and found that many other teachers faced the same situation. For many students, "harder work" was just hard. Later, when I accepted a job teaching graduate students at a university, my students asked me why students were so resistant to more challenging work. So I turned my attention to the topic of rigor and what that would look like in the classroom.

However, the issue of how to convince students to persist with challenging tasks continued to face teachers I worked with. A continuing question from teachers across the world was: "How do I help my students be successful when they are facing struggling in learning?" As one Australian teacher said, "Can struggle ever be productive?"

That's the question I answer in this book. First, let's set some parameters. Productive struggle is an opportunity for students to participate in a structured instructional situation in which they adapt current knowledge to solve a novel problem. Notice it is a structured situation. You don't just throw students into a task and allow them to struggle. Productive struggle occurs when it is a part of overall instruction. A piece of the puzzle is scaffolding. There will be times you will need to provide support for students, and that is acceptable. You just won't do the work for them.

There is some discussion on the difference between scaffolded complexity and scaffolded struggle. Scaffolded complexity focuses on increasing the content, skills, and tasks become more complex while scaffolded struggle is pointed toward the productive learning struggle itself. Although I do not use these terms, you will find that I discuss how to scaffold the content, and how to scaffold the process, especially the dispositions needed for productive struggle.

Students also take what they know and use it to solve something new. Connections are key. We learn best when we build on a base, and that's what productive struggle does.

I'd like to take a moment to address how I used artificial intelligence in my writing. I was originally very reluctant to use any AI tools, but over time, I have learned that if I take what is in my head and use it to build a prompt, Chat GPT can help spark ideas for me. Throughout the book, I used it to help me build examples for a variety of subjects and grade levels. There were also times it helped me build a set of student responses. Please note I created the specific parameters of what I was looking for so it could generate an effective response. I then took the content and wrote it in my own words. While I didn't use it for the actual writing, I wanted to be transparent about finding it to be a helpful brainstorming tool for finding ideas in various areas.

I always view books as a journey—one in which you visit different aspects of a topic and learn from each. That's what I strive to provide for you. You'll find practical examples throughout the book, and questions that allow you to process your learning. I'd love to hear your experiences, if you'd like to share both the exciting examples and the frustrating ones. You can contact me with those or with questions through my website, drblackburn.us. Enjoy your journey!

1

The Basics of Productive Struggle

Introduction

One day, I was discussing education with my dad. He told me the best definition of the purpose of education he ever heard came from a third grade teacher. She said, "the purpose of education is for students to learn what to do when they don't know what to do." My dad explained that to him, it perfectly sums up learning. If you think about it, almost everything we do requires us to figure out what to do when we don't know what to do. Start a new job? Figure out what to do. Car breaks down? Solve the problem. Decide what to do after graduation? Determine what to do next.

That third-grade teacher's definition describes school, work, and life. And for us, is encapsulates the heart of productive struggle. Practicing how to struggle through a new learning situation is exactly what prepares us for the future.

In this chapter, we'll begin by looking at myths related to productive struggle, define productive struggle, and turn our attention to the rationale for including productive struggle in our classroom. Then, we'll examine the research base and the philosophical base for productive struggle. We'll finish with a road map for the remainder of this book.

> Myths
> Definition
> Rationale
> Research Base
> Philosophical Base
> Road Map

Myths Related to Productive Struggle

Too often, we have misconceptions about productive struggle. I spoke with one researcher who said, "There's nothing good about productive struggle. You're just being mean and punishing students with hard work." I understood his perspective—productive struggle can be misused or used inappropriately. Let's look at five key myths about productive struggle.

1. Productive struggle only is for the math classroom.
2. Students don't need any prior knowledge for productive struggle.
3. Students should struggle forever with no support.
4. There is no need to plan for productive struggle.
5. The harder the struggle, the better.

Productive Struggle Is Only for the Math Classroom

First, productive struggle is appropriate for any learning classroom, from the very youngest ages to the highest grade levels. It is also suitable for any subject area. You'll find examples throughout this book ranging from math and science to language arts and social studies to art, technology, physical education, foreign language, music and more. This myth tends to be popular because there has been an emphasis on productive struggle in the math classroom, especially through national standards.

Students Don't Need Any Prior Knowledge for Productive Struggle

Next, effective productive struggle opportunities build on students' prior knowledge. Students learn best when they can connect new knowledge to existing knowledge. In other words, "hooking" the old and new loops together is most effective. This is particularly true when they are struggling with learning.

Students Should Struggle Forever With No Support

This is probably the most dangerous myth. Struggle can be a positive part of learning, but too much struggle is detrimental to learning. This is true for all students, even your advanced learners. For example, I recently decided to learn a new hobby. I chose crochet, since my grandmother was a crocheter. I was doing well, then I hit a bump. I went back to the instructions but became more frustrated. Nothing I did worked. Then my husband suggested I ask for help from a Facebook group I'm in. Within an hour, I had four options to try and was immediately able to move forward. There's nothing effective about simply throwing students into an activity without support. The trick is to balance when you provide support, how much support you provide, and equipping students to ask for support only when needed. We'll explore this in Chapter 5.

There Is No Need to Plan for Productive Struggle

Planning opportunities for productive struggle is critical. The most effective productive struggle learning experiences are carefully planned, crafting the levels and types of struggle available, equipping students with the scaffolding skills they can use when they struggle, and building in self-assessment and metacognitive opportunities for students. We'll be discussing the aspects of effective productive struggle in Chapters 3, 4, 5, and 6.

The Harder the Struggle, the Better

With productive struggle, we are looking at complexity more than just difficulty level. For example, it may be difficult to solve a math problem in which you multiply two six digit numbers. However, that's still basic computation. Creating an alternative to the Pythagorean Theorem is far more complex and requires much more thinking. We'll spend Chapter 4 discussing how to determine the appropriate level of struggle.

Defining Productive Struggle

As you can see from the myths, there are misconceptions related to productive struggle. Therefore, it's important for us to clearly understand what productive struggle is. First, let's turn our attention to the National Council of Teachers of Mathematics. Productive struggle is a part of their national standards. In their supporting research guide (2017, p. 72), they turn to Hiebert and Wearne (2003), who point out that students need to be "given opportunities to wrestle with mathematical situations that are problematic to them but within their reach."

Explore Learning, in "What is Productive Struggle?", frames the concept similarly, noting that when students master content, it leads to "deep conceptual understanding and procedural fluency that transfers to new situations and persists over time."

In *Examining Productive Failure, Productive Success, Unproductive Failure, and Unproductive Success in Learning*, Manu Kapur points out that "productive success involves structuring problem solving and learning activities with the goal of achieving both improved performance on problem solving and sustainable learning" (p. 289).

Tom Thibodeau in *What is Productive Struggle* (2024) explains that productive struggle is a concept best described as a person's ability to work through a problem to find a solution or complete a task (par. 2). Getting it isn't always easy, but in reality, learning will be more profound if our students have to work a bit harder to build their knowledge and skills. He also notes that productive struggle is not a new concept, which we'll discuss later in this chapter.

Finally, Jami Witherell, writing for the Goyen Institute in *Embracing Productive Struggle: Why It's Essential for Literacy Learning*, explains it simply (par. 4):

> Productive struggle happens when students face a challenge that's just tough enough to make them think, but not so hard that they shut down. It's that sweet spot where learning happens. It's when they push through the discomfort and find the solution on their own.

Let's look at the commonalities. First, all of the examples focus on learning, particularly new situations. Second, appropriate struggle is inherent in the process. Third, implied throughout the definitions is that the learning situation is planned.

As I've worked with productive struggle, I've found we can use a clear, thorough, teacher-friendly definition as we move forward.

> Productive struggle is an opportunity for students to participate in a structured instructional situation in which they adapt current knowledge to solve a novel problem.

There are several key words and phrases in my definition. First is student participation. You simply can't have productive struggle without students participating in the process. Next, it is a structured instructional situation. Generally, teachers plan and craft the opportunity for students to apply prior knowledge in a new situation at a level which requires the right level of struggle—not too little, not too much. We'll address this in

Chapter 4. Finally, students are using the knowledge they already have, just to something that is new to them. Connecting the two is an intricate part of productive struggle.

Why Is Productive Struggle Important?

There are four broad reasons to incorporate productive struggle in our instruction.

> **Rationale for Productive Struggle**
> 1. strengthen learning;
> 2. enhance the brain;
> 3. improve social and emotional skills;
> 4. prepare to work.

Strengthen Learning

As we explore how productive struggle impacts your classroom, it's important to realize that it strengthens student learning. Not only can it promote retention, it can also deepen overall understanding (Sriram, 2020). Additionally, Manu Kapur explains that there is a "growing body of evidence that generating solutions to novel problems prior to instruction can help students learn better from the instruction" (p. 292).

> **Sample Research**
>
> *Quasiexperimental Studies*
> Schwartz & Bransford, 1998
> Schwartz & Martin, 2004
>
> *Controlled Experimental Studies*
> DeCaro & Rittle-Johnson, 2012
> Loibl & Rummel, 2013, 2014
> Roll et al., 2011
> R. A. Schmidt & Bjork, 1992
> Schwartz et al., 2011

Enhance the Brain

There are several ways the brain is impacted by productive struggle. The staff at ST Math explain that "our brains are designed to adapt and grow through challenges." Difficult tasks such as productive struggle strengthen neural connections and enhance cognitive abilities. Rishi Sriram (2020) shares four specific brain benefits of productive struggle.

1. Building stronger neural pathways. The more a student struggles in a healthy way and overcomes challenges, the stronger these pathways become. Neuroplasticity is how our brains grow and adapt.
2. Engaging working memory. Productive struggle taps into working memory (holds and processes info ono the spot). When students are faced with a literacy task just beyond their comfort zone, they're forced to pull from what they already know, apply that knowledge, and then make sense of the new information.
3. Gaining a dopamine reward. Overcoming a challenge releases dopamine in the brain (feel good chemical).
4. Encoding for long-term learning. When students struggle productively, their brains work harder to encode that information into long-term memory.

Improve Social and Emotional Skills

Productive struggle can also improve students' social and emotional skills. For example, *Effortful Practice* authors explain that productive struggle helps students with goal-setting, planning of strategies, and monitoring their own progress, which includes students knowing when and how to ask for help. Additionally, Ellie Cowen (2016) shares that perseverance and effort are a key part of productive struggle. Finally, Rishi Sriram (2020) notes that both resilience and growth mindset can expand with productive struggle. We will address all these areas in more depth in Chapter 2.

Prepare to Work

Productive struggle can also help prepare students for the workforce. Simply moving into the workforce is a struggle for many students, so having practiced that skill is helpful. For example, according to the UK Editorial Board at Indeed, an international job search site, struggles may include time management, collaboration, work-life balance and communication (https://uk.indeed.com/career-advice/career-development/struggle-at-work). When students engage in productive struggle, they must manage their time and effectively communicate and collaborate with other students.

For their 2025 Future of Jobs Report, (https://reports.weforum.org/docs/WEF_Future_of_Jobs_Report_2025.pdf), the World Economic Forum's surveyed 100 of the largest employers in the world. Four of their top ten ranked workforce skills can be a regular part of productive struggle, especially when you craft effective opportunities.

> #4 creative thinking;
> #5 resilience, flexibility, and agility;
> #6 curiosity;
> #9 analytical thinking.

The World Economic Forum also noted that 39% of the key skills required for work will change by 2030. In other words, many key work skills don't even exist today for current sixth graders.

What Is the Research Base for Productive Struggle?

There is some discussion as to how much research supports productive struggle. Although there is not a large base of research specific to the strategy of productive strategy, we can be informed by research on the elements of productive struggle, which we will discuss in more detail in Chapter 3. My "go-to" for research is the bank of meta-analyses by John Hattie (https://visible-learning.org/hattie-ranking-influences-effect-sizes-learning-achievement/). John synthesizes research studies to identify practices that make the most impact on students.

In his newest work, John Hattie with Douglas Fisher et al. (2024) classifies the rankings from his meta-analyses using the analogy of a thermometer. Effect sizes lower than 0 are "cold," meaning they have a negative impact on achievement. Effect sizes from 0–0.4 are "cool," or they positively affect achievement. Finally, those .5 or above are "hot," which represents effects with above average impact.

Using John's work, I've divided identified effective research practice strategies into two categories: practices the teacher drives, and those in which the students participate and are responsible for. I've provided the practice, and the effect size. These are grouped by similarities rather than effect size.

Teacher practices of having appropriately challenging goals, integrating prior knowledge, using constructivist teaching, and problem-solving teaching all lend themselves to a lesson that incorporates productive struggle. For students, using effort, evaluation and reflection, and collaborative learning support productive learning. Both these teacher and student

Teacher Practices and Student Responsibilities

Teacher Practices	Students' Responsibilities
.9 teacher expectations high for all	.77 effort
.85 teacher clarity	.75 evaluation and reflection
.64 organization of instruction	.56 concentration, persistence, engagement
.68 learning goals	.48 questioning
.59 appropriately challenging goals	1.23 student expectations
.64 interpretations based on assessment of student learning	.75 elaboration and organization
	.59 elaborative interrogation
	.54 strategy monitoring
.88 ensure students understand the criteria of success	.81 self-judgement and reflection
.93 integration with prior knowledge	.52 meta-cognitive strategies
.94 prior ability	.85 organizing and transforming notes
.96 teaching students to drive their learning	.74 reciprocal teaching
.47 small group	.5 study skills
.82 class discussion	.82 classroom discussion
.5 inquiry based teaching	.62 concept mapping
.92 constructivist teaching	.58 self-verbalization and self-questioning
.44 inductive teaching	
.29 cognitive task analysis	.45 collaborative learning
.68 problem solving teaching	.62 graphic organizers and concept maps
.52 self-regulation learning	
.82 scaffolding	
.46 providing examples and guided practice	

examples, as well as the other in the table, can be used in other aspects of classroom instruction, but they are particularly pertinent with productive struggle. Again, we'll be looking at these in more detail in Chapter 3.

What Is the Philosophical Base for Productive Struggle?

The field of education has a wide range of educational philosophers. When I was in college, I was required to write my own philosophy, based on other philosophies. I ultimately synthesized parts of existing philosophies and added my own perspective. Although I've added in new pieces, my philosophy today is still reflective of that writing. When researching productive struggle, I went back to that process. I reviewed educational philosophers and pulled the aspects that support productive struggle. In this section, you'll find that productive struggle is representative of a variety of philosophers in education. My source for this entire section is *Learning Theories Simplified . . . and How to Apply Them to Teaching*, third edition by Bob Bates. I highly recommend the book as a comprehensive source of information about educational philosophers.

Educational Philosophers

Jean-Jacques Rousseau

Jean Piaget

Jerome Bruner

John Dewey

Paolo Freire

Edward Tolman

Lev Vygostsky

Norman Doidge

Renate and Geoffrey Caine

Logan Fiorella and Richard E. Mayer

Barak Rosenshine

Leslie Curzon

Carol Dweck

Michael Shayer and Phillip Adey

Robin Alexander

For example, from Jean-Jacques Rousseau we find that people should be able to learn what they want to learn and that teaching should be based on discovery enriched with the teacher guidance.

In addition to his four stages of development, Jean Piaget also posits that learners should be encouraged to learn from their peers and that learners should be allowed to learn from their mistakes. Learning from mistakes is especially important in productive struggle.

Jerome Bruner continues the focus on learning. He specifically recommends that students are allowed to discover new material to be covered so they can connect with their own understanding. This points to the very nature of discovery learning in productive struggle.

Next, John Dewey teaches us that, rather than communicating knowledge and skills but the role of a teacher is to use their learner's experiences as a teaching tool. Additionally, the challenge in providing experience-based lessons is to provide quality experiences that result in creativity and growth. Teachers must also provide guidance to learners in their use of observation and judgment. Each of these recommendations supports our use of productive struggle.

Paulo Freire gives us the concept of critical consciousness. The five step process is helpful as we develop situations for productive struggle.

1. identify the problem;
2. find an original way of representing the problem;
3. see the problem through your learner's eyes;
4. analyze the cause of the problem;
5. take action to solve the problem.

One of Edward Tolman's key principles is that learning is always purposeful and goal directed. That's important because students typically don't apply their learning unless they have a reason to do so. During productive struggle, the natural result is that students apply their learning.

Lev Vygotsky provides a key idea related to productive struggle: learning occurs in the zone of proximal development, the optimal level of difficulty. We will focus on this in Chapter 4.

Norman Doidge builds on the work of Vygotsky's level of challenge. He discusses the considering the concept of brain plasticity in order to ensure teaching has the right balance of challenge and support.

Renate and Geoffrey Caine point out the brain is a living system. Learning is enhanced by challenge, but is inhibited by threat, therefore it is critical to provide the right level of challenge in students' opportunities for productive struggle.

Logan Fiorella and Richard E. Mayer promote 8 learning strategies under the framework of the Generative Learning Theory. All of these are useful as students are working through the process of productive struggle.

> ### *Eight Learning Strategies*
> 1. learning by summarizing;
> 2. learning by mapping;
> 3. learning by drawing;
> 4. learning by imagining;
> 5. learning by self-testing;
> 6. learning by self-explaining;
> 7. learning by teaching;
> 8. learning by enacting.

Barak Rosenshine notes two crucial aspects that are essential to productive struggle: Have high expectations of your students and provide scaffolding for difficult tasks.

Leslie Curzon fleshes out our philosophy by discussing motivation. If we set goals for students that are too hard or too easy, we undermine motivation (Chapter 2).

Carol Dweck added to the philosophical base when she posited that there is a difference between a fixed mindset and a growth mindset. Students with a fixed mindset believe they are smart or not and cannot change. On the other hand, students with a growth mindset believe that, with effort, they can change and grow. A growth mindset is essential to productive struggle.

Michael Shayer and Phillip Adey detail the concept of cognitive acceleration. As we consider productive struggle, notice how these points reinforce productive struggle that promotes student learning.

Cognitive Acceleration

- If learners are given a challenge without preparation they will fail the task.
- If teachers give the answers learners may remember the facts.
- If learners develop the answers themselves they will understand.
- If learners are then encouraged to discuss how they could apply their thinking process they have undertaken to other areas, then they "become cleverer."

Finally, Robin Alexander's extensive writings demonstrate the effectiveness of dialogue in the classroom. She also focuses on working in groups and building on other students' ideas. Each of these are aspects of effective productive struggle.

Road Map to Book

I always consider reading a book to be a journey . . . a journey of learning. As we move forward, we'll be exploring the following areas. You'll also find practical examples for middle and high school in math, science, social studies, English/language arts as well as many of the specialty areas such as foreign language, technology, and art.

	Areas to Explore
Chapter 2: Student Motivation and Learning Dispositions	We'll focus on student motivation, especially intrinsic motivation, and then turn to the learning dispositions students display during productive struggle.
Chapter 3: Instruction for Productive Struggle	With a focus on instruction, we'll address general principles, the before-during-after process of instruction, and teacher and student behaviors for productive struggle.
Chapter 4: What is the Right Level for Productive Struggle?	In addition to discussing Vygotsky and Csikszentmihalyi, we'll look at leveled texts and a variety of appropriately leveled productive struggle tasks.
Chapter 5: Scaffolding for Productive Struggle	Filled with suggestions for general scaffolding, this chapter also revisits tasks from Chapter Four and adds appropriate scaffolding suggestions.
Chapter 6: Assessment in the Productive Struggle Classroom	We'll explore formative and summative assessment for the process of productive struggle, then turn our attention to formative and summative assessment for the content of productive struggle.
Chapter 7: Common Concerns about Productive Struggle	We'll address the issues of working with special needs students, learned helplessness, communicating with parents and families, and organizing for productive struggle.
Chapter 8: Collaborating for Productive Struggle	We'll discuss ways teachers can work together to consistently implement productive struggle in their classrooms.

A Final Note

Although there are many myths about productive struggle, ultimately, productive struggle is an opportunity for students to participate in a structured instructional situation in which they adapt current knowledge to solve a novel problem. There is both a research base and a philosophical foundation for incorporating productive struggle in your classroom.

Points to Ponder

1. Which myth resonates with you? Why?
2. How did you respond when you read the definition of productive struggle?
3. Which parts of the research base match what you do in your classroom?
4. What aspects of the philosophical foundation do you agree with?

Continue the Learning

Use the QR Code to access videos for your own use or for group professional development.

2
Student Motivation and Learning Dispositions

Now that we've looked at the overall base of information related to productive struggle, we need to turn our attention to two areas that are critically connected: student motivation and learning dispositions.

Many teachers tell me, "my students just aren't motivated," which is a major concern for productive struggle. After all, if students aren't motivated now, how will you convince them to attempt to do work that requires struggle? If you've read *Motivating Struggling Learners: 10 Strategies to Build Student Success,* you know that I believe all students are motivated, just not necessarily by the things we would like. Many of our students are not motivated by a desire to learn; rather, they are motivated by the approval of their friends or something else in their lives. As we start this chapter, we're going to briefly address extrinsic motivation, then turn our attention to intrinsic motivation.

Motivation

Extrinsic and Intrinsic Motivation

There are two main types of motivation: extrinsic and intrinsic. Extrinsic motivation includes all the outside ways we try to influence a student, such as rewards, stickers, or points. Intrinsic motivation comes from within the student. With extrinsic rewards, we can get temporary results, but for long-term impact, we need to help students activate their intrinsic motivation.

It's similar to looking at the ocean. I enjoy watching the waves, but when doing so I only sees the surface. I can't see the perilous undercurrents. Similarly, extrinsic motivation looks good, but we don't notice the dangers. The true beauty of the ocean is underneath the surface. As we go deeper there are beautiful marine creatures, fish, and coral. Instead of short-lived waves, I can see long-lasting beauty. And that is intrinsic motivation.

Extrinsic Motivation

Extrinsic motivation is that which comes from outside an student; anything that is external.

> ### *Examples of Extrinsic Rewards*
> Points
> Stickers
> Grades
> Library or homework passes
> Extra credit

Positive Aspects of Extrinsic Motivation

Some authors, such as Alfie Kohn, believe there is never an appropriate use for external motivation, whether for children or students. Based on my experiences, I believe there are appropriate uses for it. For example, I agree with Daniel Pink, author of *Drive*, who compares extrinsic motivation to caffeine, noting it gets you going (although you are less motivated later). Especially when students are beginning the process of productive struggle, extrinsic may be a good jumpstart.

Larry Ferlazzo in *Self-Driven Learning* also points out that everyone needs some baseline rewards, such as a clean classroom, a caring student, engaging lessons, and fair grading, in order to be motivated to learn. And Daniel Pink also points out that extrinsic rewards do work for a short time for mechanical, rote tasks, which may be needed prior to productive struggle activities.

Negative Aspects of Extrinsic Motivation

> ### *Negative Aspects of Extrinsic Motivation*
> Temporary/constant increase of reward
> Decreases intrinsic motivation

There is, however, a downside to extrinsic motivation. The results are most often temporary. To keep students motivated, while relying on extrinsic motivation, you must continue to increase the reward. A student I spoke with explained "I had a reward box where students could choose an item if they did something good. Over time, students wanted more and more . . . stickers weren't enough, then points weren't enough, then books weren't enough, etc."

Effective Ways to Use Extrinsic Motivation

"But," you may be thinking, "my students expect rewards. I can't just not use them!" So how can you effectively use extrinsic rewards? I think it's important to go back to Larry Ferlazzo's comments about baseline rewards. For all students, we need to provide:

- a clean, safe, caring environment;
- adequate materials and supplies;
- clear and fair instruction;
- openness to all ideas and suggestions.

It's important to address those areas during productive struggle. In addition, when using extrinsic rewards, we should emphasize the feeling that accompanies the reward, reinforcing that the true reward is how you feel about your success. In other words, move from a reward to celebrating the experience.

There are three other specific tips for using extrinsic motivation. First, when using rewards, do so unannounced. Rather than saying "if then, then this," simply choose random times to reward students. By surprising students, they are encouraged to put forth effort all the time.

Next, reward students through affirmation of their work. Give them an authentic audience who can appreciate their quality work.

Third, when you are using rewards, make them appropriate and meaningful to the student. Some students like certificates; others prefer public recognition. It's also important to be respectful of the individual. Some students do not like to be singled out in front of their peers. If you know that, find another way to praise them: a note, an individual comment, or even a look.

Intrinsic Motivation

Intrinsic motivation is that which comes from within the student. It is internal as opposed to external. With intrinsic motivation, students appreciate learning for its own sake. They enjoy learning and the feelings of accomplishment that accompany the activity, and that is key to productive struggle. There are many benefits to intrinsic motivation.

The Foundational Elements of Intrinsic Motivation

Intrinsic motivation has two foundational elements: People are more motivated when they value what they are doing and when they believe they have a chance for success. Students see value in a variety of ways, but the main three are relevance, autonomy, and relationships.

Value

Students typically see value through the relevance of the tasks they are asked to do, whether that is completing a word problem that includes their dogs, or understanding how the lesson is related to a hobby, such as skateboarding. In fact, most students have a streaming music station playing in their heads, WII-FM—what's in it for me? As you develop tasks and activities for productive struggle, you'll want to think about the relevance of what students are doing. When students do see value in their learning, they are more motivated to push through when the work requires struggle.

Next, there is value in the autonomy a student has. I've talked to students who say, "I'm told what to do, how to do it, and when to do it! I'm a student and I know what I am doing. When do I get to decide something?" That is actually a fairly common perception from students. Although there are some non-negotiables you deal with, if you will find options for students to make decisions, you can encourage autonomy and intrinsic motivation.

> ***Ways to Increase Student Autonomy During Productive Struggle***
>
> Offer choice of books and resources
> Give different ways to complete the productive struggle task
> Agree to students' views on how to demonstrate understanding
> Allow options of what to do when students finish their work
> Provide opportunities for students to choose partners

Finally, students find value in their relationships, with you and their peers. I once heard a speaker say that teacher and peer relationships are foundational to everything else that happens in the school. That is true. The old adage, "they don't care what you know until they know how much you care" is true. Students need to feel liked, cared for, and respected by their leaders. Many students also need the same from their peers. If they feel isolated from other students, they are disengaged and less likely to see value in what they are doing.

Success

Students are also motivated when they believe they have a chance to be successful. And that belief is built on four building blocks: level of challenge, experiences, encouragement, and views about success.

First, the degree of alignment between the difficulty of an activity and a student's skill level is a major factor in self-motivation. Imagine that you enjoy playing soccer, and you have the chance to compete in a local game. You will be playing against Lionel Messi (Miami), named World Player of the Year a record eight times. How do you feel? In that situation, there's plenty of opportunity for challenge, probably too much challenge! Or perhaps you love reading stories, but the only language you can read is Spanish. How motivated will you be in a literature class? For optimal motivation, the activity should be challenging but in balance with your ability to perform. Part of your job as a teacher is to determine if a student is struggling, and if so, provide appropriate support. On the other hand, if one of your students is not challenged, look for ways to give them an opportunity to try a new challenge. Productive struggle is the perfect way to provide challenge, and we'll spend Chapter 4 discussing how to determine the right level of challenge.

A student's experiences are an important factor to their success with productive struggle. A student is more likely to believe they can be successful if they have been successful in the past. Conversely, if they have a pattern of failing, they will struggle with motivation.

A third building block to feelings of success is the encouragement a student receives from others. Encouragement is "the process of facilitating the development of the person's inner resources and courage towards positive movement" (Dinkmeyer & Losoncy, 1992, p. 16).

When you encourage, you accept students as they are, so they will accept themselves. You value and reinforce attempts and efforts and help them realize that mistakes are learning tools. Encouragement says, "Try, and try again. You can do it. Go in your own direction, at your own pace. I believe in you." Encouragement can be in the form of words, but you can also provide encouragement through a consistent, positive presence in your students' lives.

It's also important for students to read and learn about people who failed before they succeeded, because the final building block is a student's views about success and failure. Many students see failure as the end rather than as an opportunity to learn before trying again. But there are countless examples, from Abraham Lincoln to Steve Jobs, of people who have experienced failure in their lives, only to become successful. How we define success and failure drives many of your students' beliefs about your own ability to succeed.

Planning for Motivation	
Aspect of Intrinsic Motivation	*How I'll Build This Into Productive Struggle*
Value: relevance	
Value: autonomy	
Value: relationships	
Success: challenge	
Success: experiences	
Success: encouragement	
Success: view	

Learning Dispositions

Now that we've discussed the broad concepts of motivation, I want us to turn our attention to the dispositions students display. As I researched productive struggle, it became clear that, which academic skills are critical, so are the learning dispositions that students have. These tend to fit under the broader concept of motivation. Although they are sometimes called thinking skills, soft skills, or non-academic skills, learning dispositions is a better descriptor for what we want. These are the mental attitudes and skills that students have (and can improve upon) that help them solve the problems that occur in productive struggle. First, let's review some related research, then discuss my five dispositions for productive struggle. That section will include practical strategies for encouraging each disposition in your classroom. Please note those are not productive struggle activities; they are activities which allow students to practice particular dispositions.

Related Research and Theories

Costa and Kallick

First, Arthur Costa and Bena Kallick (2008) address their perspective on Habits of Mind. These are dispositions for intelligent behavior and support problem-solving and lifelong learning. As they point out, their identified list is focused on "thinking dispositions, or tendencies toward particular patterns of intellectual behavior" (p. 19).

Sixteen Habits of Mind

1. persisting;
2. managing impulsivity;
3. listening with understanding and empathy;
4. thinking flexibly;
5. thinking about thinking (metacognition);
6. striving for accuracy;
7. questioning and posing problems;
8. applying past knowledge to new situations;
9. thinking and communicating with clarity and precision;
10. gathering data through all senses;
11. creating, imagining, innovating;
12. responding with wonderment and awe;
13. taking responsible risks;
14. finding humor;
15. thinking interdependently;
16. remaining open to continuous learning.

Claxton

Guy Claxton's Learning Power Approach (LPA) identifies mental ingredients that make up learning power, which can be built, just as muscle power can be built. As Guy points out, "the approach is to develop all students as confident and capable learners—ready, willing, and able to choose, design, research, pursue, troubleshoot, and evaluate learning for themselves, alone and with others, in school or out (p. 40)." His list also encompasses other embedded areas.

> Curiosity
> Attention
> Determination
> Imagination
> Thinking
> Socializing
> Reflection
> Organization

Wagner

Tony Wagner, the author of *The Global Achievement Gap* (2008) takes a different approach. He focuses on thinking skills that are necessary to survive in life, but particularly in the workforce. He considers the identified dispositions as survival skills. "Indeed, the 7 survival skills are for future generations what the 'Three Rs' were for previous generations. They are the 'new basic skills' for work, learning, and citizenship in the 21st century" (p. 42).

Seven Survival Skills

1. critical thinking and problem solving;
2. collaboration across networks and leading by influence;
3. agility and adaptability;
4. initiative and entrepreneurialism;
5. effective oral and written communication;
6. accessing and analyzing information;
7. curiosity and imagination.

Ritchhart

In 2002, Ron Ritchhart released a book on intellectual character. His main focus, that education should shape intellectual character, included information on using dispositions to build character, which will encourage critical and reflective thinking. As he describes it,

> What does intelligence look like in action? What are the qualities of thought and characteristics of mind we expect to see when someone is acting intelligently? What are the patterns of behavior and attitudes that we associate with someone who acts smart?
> (p. 13)

He notes that intelligence is not something you possess as much as how you perform. Dispositions are critical to that.

Dispositions

1. Creative thinking: looking out, up, around, and about
    - open-minded
    - curious
2. Reflective thinking: looking within
    - metacognitive
3. Critical thinking: looking at, through, and in between
    - seeking truth and understanding
    - strategic
    - skeptical

Australian Girls in STEM Toolkit

Finally, I turned to Australia for a different perspective, although one with common themes.

The Girls in STEM Toolkit (the GiST) focuses on providing girls and young women with resources to help them understand how their existing skills and interests can link to STEM careers and study pathways. Funded by the Australian Government Department of Industry, Science and Resources and managed by Education Services Australia, it provides a range of helpful tools for teachers.

Their work with dispositions is founded on the belief that having a growth mindset is important for girls to move forward with STEM studies and careers. Specific dispositions can be evidenced by behaviors in the classroom.

- curiosity and scepticism (skepticism);
- collaboration;
- creativity;
- persistence;
- problem-solving;
- intellectual risk-taking;
- making connections.

https://www.thegist.edu.au/educators/create-inclusive-classrooms/talk-tools-build-stem-capital/foster-stem-dispositions/

Dispositions for Productive Struggle

Based on the previous information, I synthesized and coordinated the dispositions into a simple set of five general dispositions that are needed in a productive struggle classroom.

Curiosity and Creative Thinking
Persistence and Self-Discipline
Strategic Problem-Solving and Metacognition
Risk-Taking
Integrating Thinking

You may be wondering why I didn't include collaboration in my list. I will address students' working together in Chapter 5, but I consider that to be more of a social skill than a disposition.

Let's look at each of these five in depth. I'll start by expanding on the disposition with more detail, share a picture of what the disposition looks like when students are starting to activate the disposition, beginning to master the disposition, then demonstrating skill with the disposition. I'll finish each section by providing subject area middle and high school examples of activities for core and related areas you can do in the classroom to foster the disposition.

Curiosity and Creative Thinking

Curiosity and creative thinking incorporates questioning, generating original ideas, and open-mindedness. This also includes that students evaluate information for bias or false information and act accordingly. In other words, they test possibilities through critical evaluation, looking for facts and evidence.

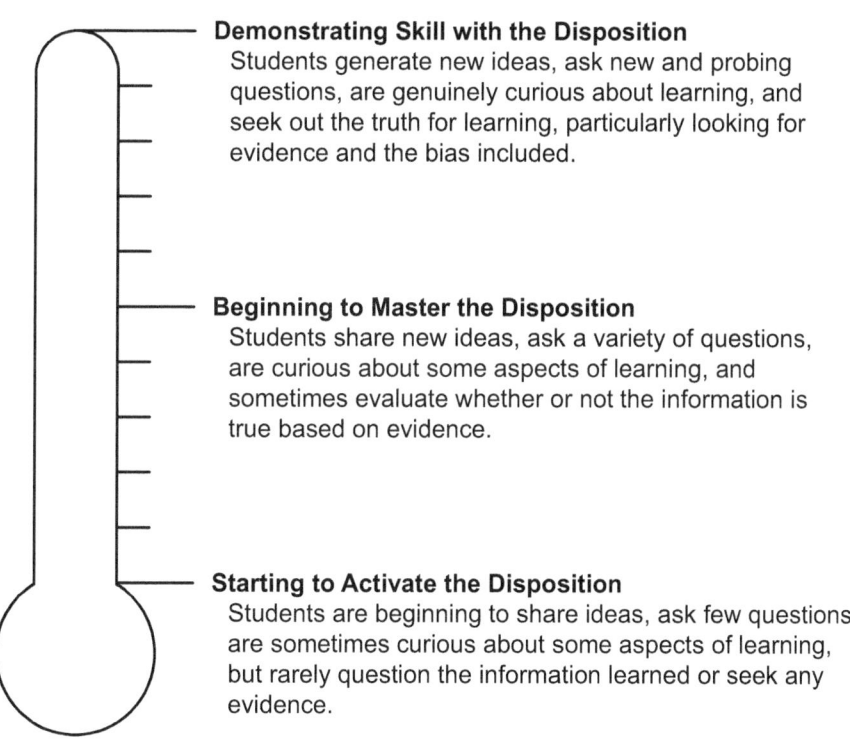

Measuring Up With Curiosity and Creative Thinking

Demonstrating Skill with the Disposition
Students generate new ideas, ask new and probing questions, are genuinely curious about learning, and seek out the truth for learning, particularly looking for evidence and the bias included.

Beginning to Master the Disposition
Students share new ideas, ask a variety of questions, are curious about some aspects of learning, and sometimes evaluate whether or not the information is true based on evidence.

Starting to Activate the Disposition
Students are beginning to share ideas, ask few questions, are sometimes curious about some aspects of learning, but rarely question the information learned or seek any evidence.

Generating Original Ideas Activity

Math

Students create a game based on a particular area of mathematics (geometry, variables, irrational numbers, etc.).

Science

After researching the issue, brainstorm solutions to reduce plastic waste and create a social media campaign to encourage reduction.

Social Studies

Choose a historical event. Imagine it had ended differently. Script and act out a drama with the alternate ending.

English/Language Arts

Choose a minor character from our novel. Build a social media profile for the character, including a series of at least 15 posts.

Foreign Languages

Write an original idiom in the assigned language.

Physical Education

Design a blended workout that meets a fitness goal.

Looking for Bias Activity

Math
Analyze a given data set for sample bias.

Science
Choose an issue related to science. Research multiple sources and identify bias.

Social Studies
Analyze two primary source materials that are related to each other. Identify and explain bias.

English/Language Arts
Critique a persuasive text for bias.

Technology
Search for an issue or topic using at least two search engines. Analyze for bias in the search results.

Art
Choose a museum and take a virtual tour. Analyze any underrepresentations.

Persistence and Self-discipline

With this disposition, students sustain effort throughout the productive learning process. They also manage their frustration when things are not going well.

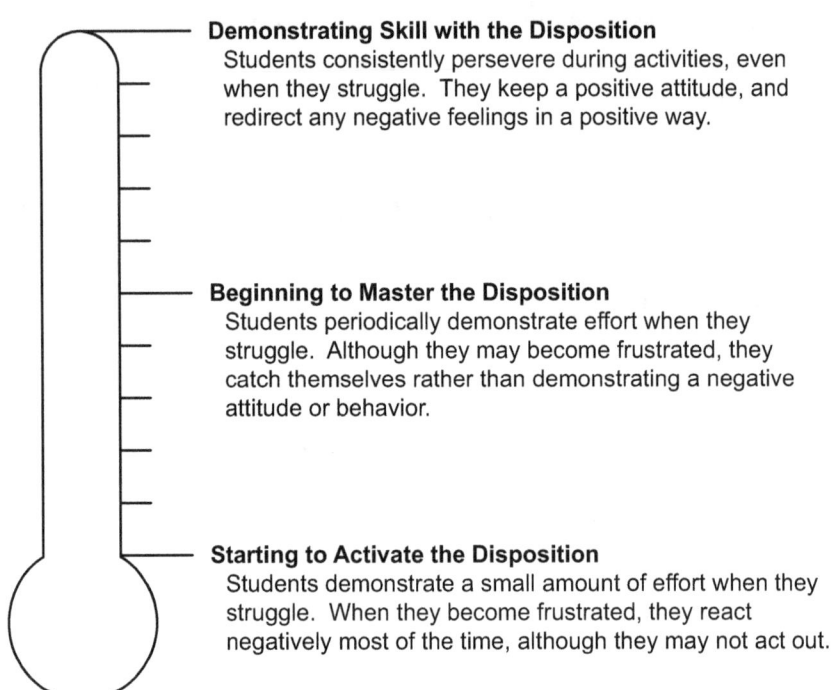

Measuring Up With Persistence and Self-discipline

Demonstrating Skill with the Disposition
Students consistently persevere during activities, even when they struggle. They keep a positive attitude, and redirect any negative feelings in a positive way.

Beginning to Master the Disposition
Students periodically demonstrate effort when they struggle. Although they may become frustrated, they catch themselves rather than demonstrating a negative attitude or behavior.

Starting to Activate the Disposition
Students demonstrate a small amount of effort when they struggle. When they become frustrated, they react negatively most of the time, although they may not act out.

Showing Effort Activity

Math

Attempt a challenging proof. When you get stuck, make notations, but make as much progress as possible.

Science

Conduct a lab experiment that requires multiple trials.

Social Studies

Students research an uncommon topic from history, persisting to find information.

English/Language Arts

Students work through several peer conferences and writing revisions.

Chorus

Students practice complex piece, requiring repeated rehearsals.

Engineering/Makerspace

Students build a prototype that requires repeated designs and redesigns.

Managing Frustration Activity

Using an anchor chart similar to the two here adapted from Chat GPT with my input, brainstorm ideas with students as to how they feel when they are frustrated and what they can do instead.

Managing Frustration	
When I feel frustrated ...	*I can ...*
When I don't understand directions	Ask teacher or another student to clarify
When it feels too hard	Chunk the steps
When I get stuck	Try a different way
When I make mistakes	Think of another time I made mistakes and then succeeded
When I am failing	Think about my past successes
When I feel like giving up	Take a breath and try again

Strategic Problem-Solving and Metacognition

Students not only use problem solving and strategic thinking skills, they also reflect on their own thinking and make appropriate adjustments in order to be successful.

Measuring Up With Strategic Problem-Solving and Metacognition

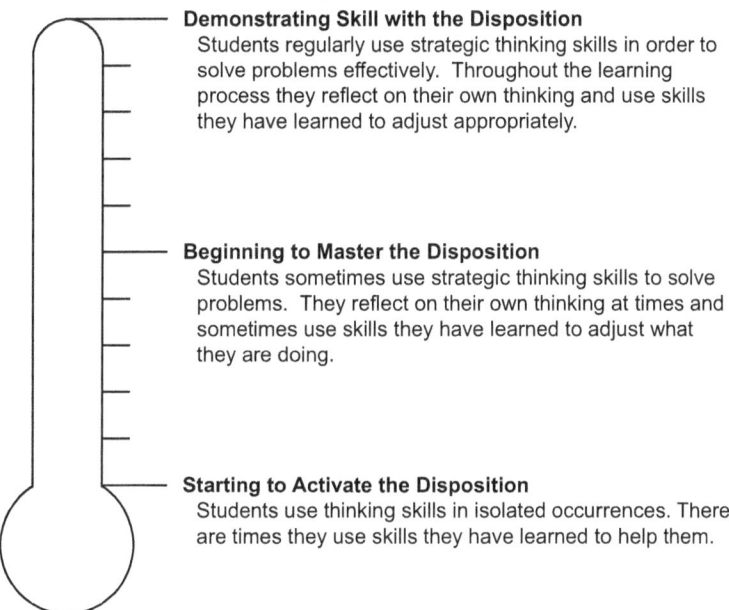

Demonstrating Skill with the Disposition
Students regularly use strategic thinking skills in order to solve problems effectively. Throughout the learning process they reflect on their own thinking and use skills they have learned to adjust appropriately.

Beginning to Master the Disposition
Students sometimes use strategic thinking skills to solve problems. They reflect on their own thinking at times and sometimes use skills they have learned to adjust what they are doing.

Starting to Activate the Disposition
Students use thinking skills in isolated occurrences. There are times they use skills they have learned to help them.

Problem-Solving Activity

Math

Students solve a non-routine problem and share their problem-solving process with a partner.

Science

Students analyze a complex set of data, such as world trends in climate.

Social Studies

Students serve as policy advisors for a particular event in history.

English/Language Arts

Students revise a flawed paragraph or essay using writing and editing strategies.

Career and Technical Education

Students devise solutions to a given workplace problem.

Debate/Speech

Students develop rebuttals to debate points.

Metacognition Activity

Math

Students reflect on why they used the strategy they chose to solve a particular problem.

Science

Students evaluate how their initial assumptions influenced their data interpretation.

Social Studies

Students reflect on how their perceptions or bias influenced their choice of solutions.

English/Language Arts

Students write a journal entry on how different metacognitive strategies helped or hinder their comprehension.

Band

Students reflect on how their role impacted the overall band performance.

Family and Consumer Sciences

Students reflect on how substitutions to a recipe impacted the final dish.

Risk-Taking

This area focuses on intellectual risk-taking. In other words, students ask questions, especially ones for which they do not know the answers. They also tolerate uncertainty and embrace mistakes as opportunities for growth.

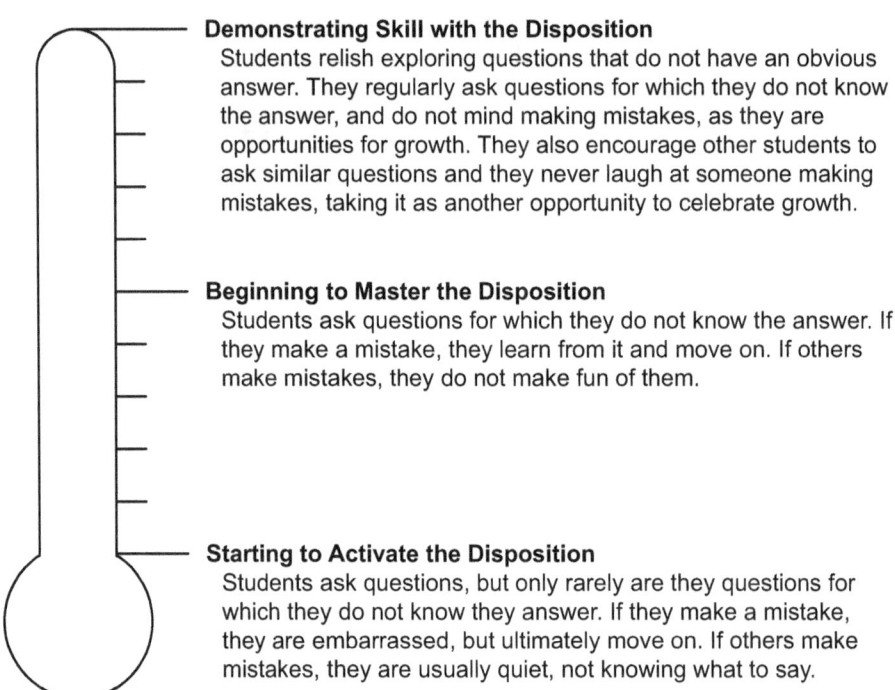

Measuring Up With Risk-Taking

Demonstrating Skill with the Disposition
Students relish exploring questions that do not have an obvious answer. They regularly ask questions for which they do not know the answer, and do not mind making mistakes, as they are opportunities for growth. They also encourage other students to ask similar questions and they never laugh at someone making mistakes, taking it as another opportunity to celebrate growth.

Beginning to Master the Disposition
Students ask questions for which they do not know the answer. If they make a mistake, they learn from it and move on. If others make mistakes, they do not make fun of them.

Starting to Activate the Disposition
Students ask questions, but only rarely are they questions for which they do not know they answer. If they make a mistake, they are embarrassed, but ultimately move on. If others make mistakes, they are usually quiet, not knowing what to say.

Tolerating Uncertainty Activity

Math

Design a proof for the Collatz Conjecture.

Science

Predict the outcome of a lab investigation with incomplete information.

Social Studies

Explore unresolved debates in history, such as the Fall of Rome.

English/Language Arts

Discuss a story with an ambiguous ending, such as *The Giver*.

Theatre/Drama

Practice improvisational scenes with random prompts.

Agricultural Education

Create farm plans with unpredictable conditions.

Uncertain Questions

You can use these questions for discussion or writing. Each is designed to be uncertain.

Math

How would math change if a number could be negative and positive at the same time?

> **Science**
>
> Could something be alive and not alive at the same time?

> **Social Studies**
>
> Can a society be truly fair to everyone?

> **English/Language Arts**
>
> Is it possible for two people to interpret a story differently and both be correct?

> **Related Areas**
>
> Foreign Language: If a word cannot be accurately translated into English, does that mean it isn't real?
>
> Technology/Computer Science: What would happen if Artificial Intelligence could feel emotions?
>
> Art: Can there be meaning in art if the artist didn't intend meaning?
>
> Chorus: Is silence part of music? How?
>
> Band: Can music exist if there is no rhythm?
>
> Physical Education: Can you be strong physically but not be healthy?
>
> Theatre/Drama: If you improvise during a play, is it still the same play?
>
> Career/Technical Education: What jobs will still exist in 20 years, given the growth of AI?
>
> Family/Consumer Sciences: If you prepare correctly, does that guarantee success?
>
> Agricultural Education: Can farming ever be completely natural?
>
> Media/Journalism: Can news ever be bias-free?
>
> Debate/Speech: Can you win a debate if no one changes their minds?
>
> Engineering/Makerspace: If you create something that works, but the design is imperfect, is that good?

Integrating Thinking

Students apply their prior knowledge, make connections, and transfer learning across lessons, texts, and/or subjects.

Measuring Up With Integrating Thinking

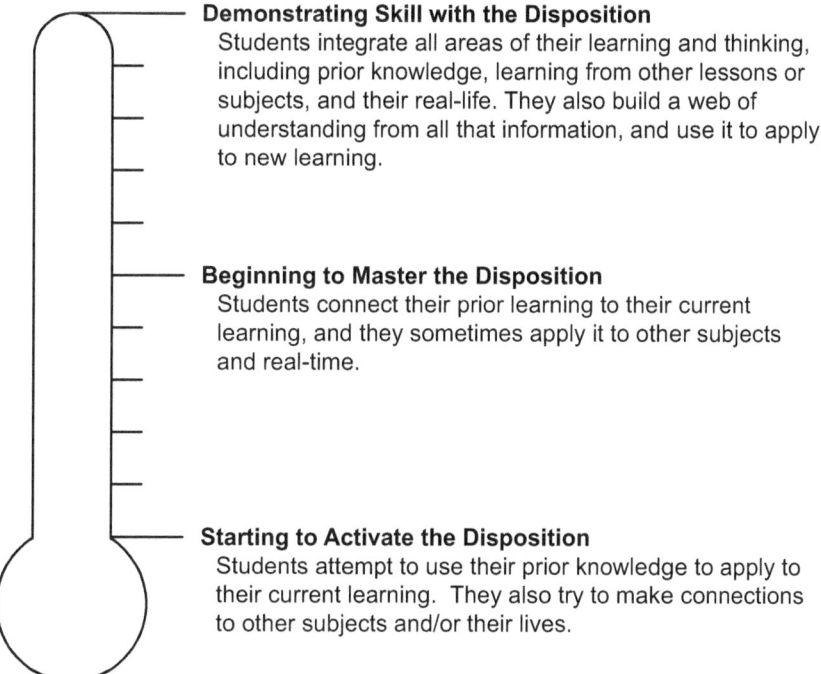

Demonstrating Skill with the Disposition
Students integrate all areas of their learning and thinking, including prior knowledge, learning from other lessons or subjects, and their real-life. They also build a web of understanding from all that information, and use it to apply to new learning.

Beginning to Master the Disposition
Students connect their prior learning to their current learning, and they sometimes apply it to other subjects and real-time.

Starting to Activate the Disposition
Students attempt to use their prior knowledge to apply to their current learning. They also try to make connections to other subjects and/or their lives.

Making Connections Activity

Math

Students apply proportional reasoning to science experiments or map scales.

Science

Link ecosystems to historical events such as the Dust Bowl.

Social Studies

Compare the American and French Revolutions to protests happening today.

English/Language Arts

Compare themes in literature such as justice and freedom to today's society.

Journalism

Compare journalistic techniques to persuasive techniques from English/Language Arts.

Technology/Computer Science

Connect problem-solving in coding to solving logic puzzles in math.

A Final Note

Student motivation impacts productive struggle, either positively or negatively, so we need to consider a student's motivation. We can temporarily impact extrinsic motivation or build a classroom environment that supports intrinsic motivation. Additionally, we need to foster five dispositions: Curiosity and Creative Thinking, Persistence and Self-Discipline, Strategic Problem-Solving and Metacognition, Risk-Taking, and Integrating Thinking.

Points to Ponder

1. How do you use extrinsic motivation in your classroom? How might you adjust your approach?
2. How can you incorporate aspects of intrinsic motivation in your classroom?
3. Which of the five dispositions would you like to focus on in your classroom?

Continue the Learning

Use the QR Code to access videos for your own use or for group professional development.

3

Instruction for Productive Struggle

The biggest question I hear about productive struggle is, "What does it look like in the classroom?" That's the question I will try to answer in this chapter. We'll start by looking at general principles for teaching productive struggle, then turn our attention to the "before-during-after process" of productive struggle, then finish with the teacher and student behaviors you see during the productive struggle process.

General Strategies for Teaching Productive Struggle

Let's start with discussing four general strategies to use when teaching productive struggle.

> Build a Climate for Productive Struggle
> Show Students What Good Looks Like
> Practice with a Partner (or Group)
> Independent Practice

Build a Climate for Productive Struggle

The first step in creating a productive struggle classroom is building a climate that will support that struggle. There are five aspects of a climate for productive struggle.

> Encourage growth mindset behaviors
> Praise risk-taking
> Applaud collaborative work
> Celebrate mistakes and redirections
> Commend perseverance and resilience

Encourage Growth Mindset Behaviors

Do your students demonstrate growth mindset behaviors? They will need those to be successful. As we discussed in Chapter 2, there are specific student beliefs and behaviors that are essential for productive struggle. These are the ones you want to teach, facilitate, and encourage in your classroom.

> Focuses on continuous learning
> Learns from mistakes
> Believes in the power of effort
> Embraces challenge

Praise Risk-Taking

Next, it's important to praise and positively reinforce those times when students take risks. This might include when a student tentatively raises his hand, or when one of your students agrees to show her work to the class, or when someone takes the lead in a group activity. For students, each of these is a risk. So is attempting a task during productive struggle. Because the task is challenging, each of your students is risking that they might fail. So it's important to praise any attempts to take a risk. Let's look at sample praise statements.

> It's great that you chose to share your answer, even though you weren't sure you were correct.
> I admire how you took the lead in our group activity.
> Way to go! I'm so proud of you for raising your hand.
> You showed outstanding effort, really focusing on how to solve the problem.

Applaud Collaborative Work

Another characteristic you want to build as a part of your climate is the role of collaborative work. Students working together, learning together, supporting and encouraging each other is critical to successful productive struggle. There are three steps to building collaborative work in your classroom: modeling collaboration, providing structured, guided practice, and reinforcing positive efforts. In other words, teach collaboration just like you would teach any other skill.

Collaborative Learning

	You're a Team Player 3	You're Working on It... 2	You're the Lone Ranger 1	Total for Each Category
G Group Dedication	I listened respectfully to my teammates' ideas and offered suggestions that helped my group.	I did listen to ideas, but I didn't give suggestions.	I was distracted and more interested in the other groups than my group.	**Group Dedication** I circled number 3 2 1
R Responsibility	I eagerly accepted responsibility with my group and tried to do my part to help everyone in my group.	I accepted responsibility within my group without arguing.	I quarreled and did not accept roles given by my group.	**Responsibility** I circled number 3 2 1
O Open Communication	I listened to others' ideas and tried to solve conflicts peacefully.	I listened to others' ideas, but did not try to solve conflicts.	I was controlling and argumentative to my group.	**Open Communication** I circled number 3 2 1

Collaborative Learning

	You're a Team Player 3	You're Working on It . . . 2	You're the Lone Ranger 1	Total for Each Category
U Use of Work Time	I was involved and engaged; I encouraged my group the entire time we were working.	I tried my best the entire time we were working.	I was not involved and did not offer any suggestions for the good of the group.	**Use of Work Time** I circled number 3 2 1
P Participation	I was a team member. I offered ideas, suggestions, and help for my group.	I participated in the project, but did not offer to help anyone.	I did not participate because I was not interested.	**Participation** I circled number 3 2 1
				Total ____

Celebrate Mistakes and Redirections

Mistakes are a normal part of a productive struggle classroom. How we handle mistakes and the students who make them matters. I was in a classroom where a student had made a minor spelling mistake in her writing. The teacher scanned the writing, criticized the spelling, and moved on to the next student. The young girl was devastated, and from that point, she was a reluctant writer. The teacher didn't understand why the student didn't try anymore, but it was due to her negative reinforcement. A better approach would have been to use a praise sandwich: praise the content, ask questions about the spelling so the student could identify and redo the mistake, and praise her overall work.

An even better approach is a Marvelous Mistakes section on your wall. A teacher in Arizona shared this with me. Anytime a student makes a mistake, provide guidance so students can correct their own mistakes. Then, post both the mistake and the correction on the wall and have everyone cheer a Marvelous Mistake.

Commend Perseverance and Resilience

Finally, focus on the times when students persevere or show resilience. As with most of the other culture elements, if you commend students on their perseverance and resilience, they will try continue those efforts. What we reinforce, we will see again. If we repeat our praise, they will repeat their positive actions.

Student Behaviors	
Commend This . . .	*Not This . . .*
Student Puts Forth Effort	Student Gives Up Before He/She Starts
Student Tries Alternatives When Something Doesn't Work	Student Stops When Something Doesn't Work
Student Learns from Mistakes	Student Gets Stuck After a Mistake
After a Bad Grade, Student Reflects on What Happened so He/She Can Learn	After a Bad Grade, Student Gives Up

Show Students What Good Looks Like

It's critical to use the gradual release model to help students succeed with productive struggle. Begin by modeling what "good" productive struggle looks like. You'll also want to think aloud during the entire process to help students understand what is happening. When I was a beginning teacher, I modeled instructional processes, but just assumed my students knew what I was thinking. I quickly learned that wasn't true. As Patrice told me one day, "I see what you are doing, but I don't know why you are doing it." That's why it's so important to share your thinking.

> So I see this diagram that shows both photosynthesis and cellular respiration. Let me think through it step by step. Photosynthesis happens in the chloroplasts of plant cells. Plants take in carbon dioxide and water, and using sunlight, they produce glucose and oxygen. I know the formula is $CO_2 + H_2O + \text{sunlight} \rightarrow C_6H_{12}O_6 + O_2$. Now, I also notice that cellular respiration is almost the reverse. In the mitochondria, glucose and oxygen are used to release energy, producing carbon dioxide and water as waste products. The equation is $C_6H_{12}O_6 + O_2 \rightarrow CO_2 + H_2O + ATP$. I'm noticing a cycle here: the outputs of photosynthesis—glucose and oxygen—are the inputs for respiration. And the outputs of respiration—carbon dioxide and water—are the inputs for photosynthesis. So, these two processes are interconnected. If I had to summarize my thinking, I'd say plants and animals depend on each other because plants provide oxygen and food, while animals (including humans) provide carbon dioxide that plants use.

Notice how, in this productive struggle scenario, you are modeling everything the students can do. You showed the importance of restating the problem, chunking information, and double-checking their work with another strategy. You also showed that uncertainty is acceptable. Students will likely still struggle but preparing them ensures the struggle is productive.

Practice With a Partner or Group

After ensuring that students understand what you have modeled, move to a partner or group task. Either is acceptable; it just depends on your students. I sometimes prefer to use partners because it is a bit more manageable, but groups of 3 or 4 also work. Let's assume we are going to do a writing task with partners. You'll begin by introducing the task, reminding them of some scaffolding strategies (Chapter 5) that may be helpful, and then providing the productive struggle task.

> Provide students a story with an incomplete ending. Their task is to develop at least two possible endings, then choose the best option. They will also need to justify (either orally or in writing) why the one they chose is best, using evidence from the story.

As you are monitoring your pairs or groups, there are several key things you may observe. I've provided some possibilities, as well as the appropriate response.

What You Observe	
What You Observe	*What You Can Do*
Students can't seem to get started.	Ask questions that help them focus on the task and the concrete actions to take.
Students are stuck choosing the best option.	Remind them to think about what they know about story elements. How can that help them choose an option?
Students are struggling to justify their choice.	Ask students if they remember how to justify an answer. How have they done it in the past?

Notice the suggestions are all facilitative. You are not solving a problem for them; you are asking them questions or guiding them to think about something that might help them complete the task. It's tempting to want to provide too much help—resist that temptation! Remember, productive struggle means there should be some struggle.

Independent Practice

Finally, you want to give students the opportunity to practice on their own. Do not move to this step until students have been somewhat successful with a partner or a group. Also, part of gradual release is determining when to move to each step of the process. We'll be discussing choosing the right level of task in Chapter 4, but here, let me make one point. If this step is the first time students are working on their own, choose something that is challenging, but not necessarily highly challenging. The purpose here is *practice*. They are learning how to do this. Before they try productive struggle individually, discuss how they might handle different aspects of the struggle. I like to use an anchor chart with questions and discuss with the class possible answers.

Anchor Chart for Students	
What if I don't know how to get started?	
What if I get stuck?	
How do I know I'm on the right track?	
How do I know if I am successful?	

Perhaps this is your next task:

> Students will analyze two primary source documents about the same historical event and analyze how the authors' perspectives differ. Students should justify the elements of their analysis with specific evidence from the text, as well as other information from their own research and our class lessons.

Provide the productive struggle prompt to students and ask them to brainstorm with a partner the answer to the questions on the anchor chart. Then, discuss possible strategies with the whole group. You might see answers similar to those in the following table.

Anchor Chart for Primary Source Documents	
What if I don't know how to get started?	Read the documents. Write a summary of each document.
What if I get stuck?	Re-read the question to see what to do. Make a checklist of what to do. Use a graphic organizer to help with information.
How do I know I'm on the right track?	Am I following the task? I might turn the task into a question and see if I can answer yes.
How do I know if I am successful?	Did I address all parts of the question or task? Can I ask someone else in the class to check my work?

As you look at the sample questions and student responses, you'll notice that students are still struggling through the process; they just discuss possible ways they can address the struggle.

Do This . . . Not That With Students

Dr. Katie Perez, curriculum specialist and former teacher from New Braunfels, Texas, recommends working with students to identify what is and is not productive. I like the headings she uses, asking students to discuss what parts of productive struggle should and should not feel and look like.

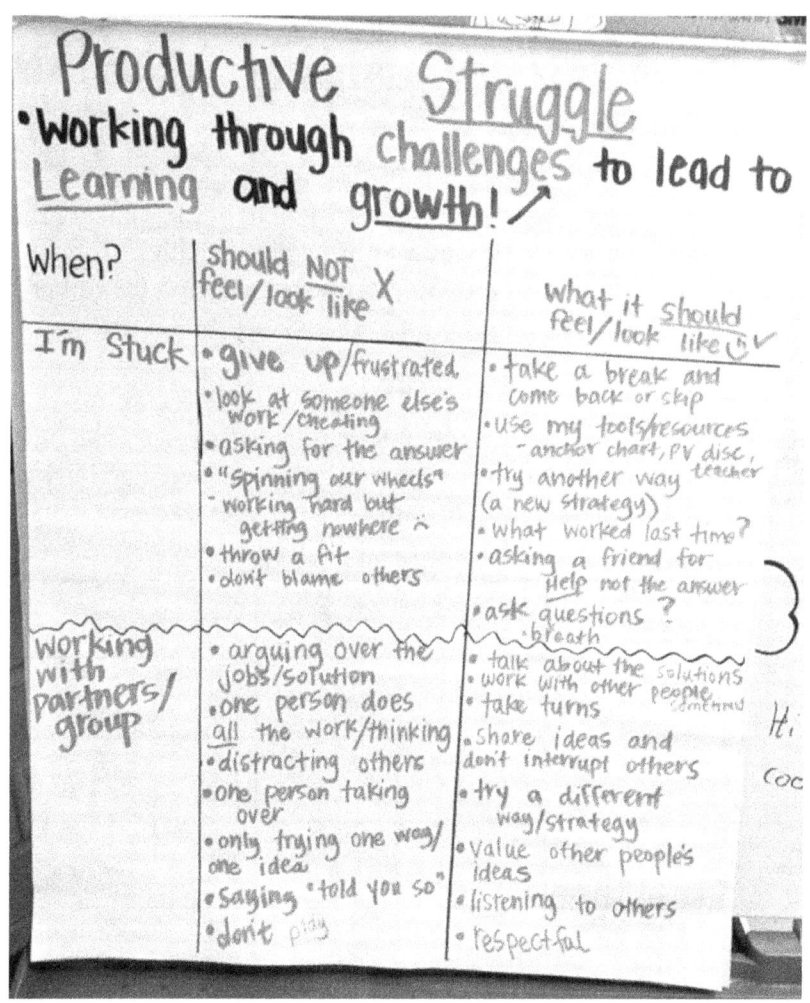

Instruction for Productive Struggle ◆ 53

Before-during-after Productive Struggle

Too often, we think of productive struggle as an isolated event rather than a part of the overall instructional process. Simply throwing students into productive struggle isn't productive—it's just struggle. Let's look at what happens before, during, and after productive struggle.

Before Productive Struggle

Before students engage in productive struggle, there are key actions we need to take as teachers.

Before Productive Struggle

Pre-assessment

Consideration of Prior Knowledge/Readiness

Planning

First, we'll need some type of pre-assessment to help us ensure that the productive struggle is effective. You might use information from a previous lesson, a short pre-test, or anticipation guide to help you gather data.

Directions

Read each of the following statements. Before we read, mark whether you think it is true or false. After we read, we'll go back and check your answers. Be ready to explain what you learned.

Statement	Before Reading (T/F)	After Reading (T/F)
1.	T ☐ F ☐	T ☐ F ☐
2.	T ☐ F ☐	T ☐ F ☐
3.	T ☐ F ☐	T ☐ F ☐
4.	T ☐ F ☐	T ☐ F ☐

Sometimes connected to the pre-assessment is the consideration of students' prior knowledge and readiness. We may have this information from previous work or assessments with students, or we may want to do a separate activity to help prepare students for the productive struggle. Many teachers use a K-W-L before a lesson, which you'll see in Chapter 6.

Then, you'll use all this information to plan your instruction. Whenever you plan, take into consideration the following aspects.

Aspects to Consider

How this lesson fits into your overall scope and sequence.

How the productive struggle activity fits into the lesson.

How the productive struggle activity addresses your standard/goal/objective.

Whether students are prepared with the needed dispositions for the activity (Chapter 2).

Whether students are prepared with any needed prerequisite knowledge.

How students are prepared for self-scaffolding (Chapter 5) if needed.

How the productive struggle activity will be structured for students.

How you will structure groups if this is a partner or group task (Chapter 5)

During Productive Struggle

Productive struggle becomes a part of your lesson. Let's look at three activities that occur during productive struggle.

During Productive Struggle

Instruction/Scaffolding

Ongoing Assessment

Adjustments

First, you have your instruction, which includes scaffolding. Your planning, which was based on what you know about your students, will provide the framework for how productive struggle fits into the overall flow of the lesson. For example, you may need to incorporate an introductory activity before productive struggle, or, based on prior lessons, you may jump right into the productive struggle task. You also may need to pre-teach particular scaffolding and metacognitive strategies. There's not a perfect time; it depends on your students' readiness.

Then, you will have the productive struggle activity itself. Sometimes we fall into linear thinking—this will happen first, this second, this third. Productive struggle is a bit more amorphous. You may set up a sequence, but the very nature of struggle means it won't necessarily go in a straight line. Different students will hit stumbling blocks and use strategies you have taught them to self-correct and move forward; others may need you to provide some guided questioning (Chapter 6). Most importantly, you may not be able to predict what will happen. With planning, you'll set up a task designed to allow them to struggle (Chapter 4), but some will react in unexpected ways. Be prepared to provide appropriate guidance, always with an eye toward student independence.

Next, you will use ongoing formative assessment (Chapter 7) to see where students are and where they are going. Formative assessment can help you identify strengths and weaknesses, and particularly help you see where you need to make adjustments. That's the third part of productive struggle, making adjustments in order to have a more productive and successful experience.

Let's look at how this might play out in the classroom.

In this high school example, the teacher needed to make adjustments to the level of the task, as the original task was too simplistic.

> ### *Sample Productive Struggle Lesson Description (Social Studies)*
>
> Students are working on a lesson on how a bill becomes a law. The teacher notices they are simply looking at bills that were successful, so the readjusts the lesson to include a focus on the obstacles that are faced, such as the bill not being assigned to a committee.

After Productive Struggle

> ### *After Productive Struggle*
> Summative Assessment
> Reflection
> Short- and Long-Term Planning

Finally, after students have completed the productive struggle activity, there are three actions for you to take. First, provide some form of summative assessment to determine what students have learned. You may decide to assess only content, or you may want to assess the productive struggle process (Chapter 6). Either is fine.

Next, you'll reflect on what you learned from the formative assessments during the lesson and the summative assessment. Did students master or show progress toward a particular objective or skill? Did they truly struggle or was the task too easy? Or, was the struggle frustrating—the task was too hard or they were unprepared?

With the following chart, you log each objective and note the percentage of your students who mastered the objective, are progressing toward the objective, or have not mastered the objective.

Content Knowledge Reflection			
Objective	*Mastered*	*Progressing*	*Not Mastered*

With the process of productive struggle, you might note broader information. You can use this as a check-off, or you can designate how many/what percentage of your students fit in each category.

Productive Struggle Process Reflection				
Task	Just Right	Too Hard		Too Easy
Needed Adjustments				
Skill			Yes	No
Students Had Appropriate Prior Knowledge				
Students Were Prepared with Self-Monitoring Skills				
Students Made Adjustments as Needed				
Students Used Scaffolding Skills				

Finally, use your reflections to plan for the future—both short term and long term. What needs to happen immediately? What do you need to do to help students be prepared in the future? Be sure to log this information so you will have it for additional planning and instruction.

Additional Reflective Notes	
Based on . . .	I Need to . . .
Content Knowledge Mastery	
Students' Skills During Productive Struggle	
The Amount of Struggle	
The Effectiveness of Struggle	
My Other Observations	

Teacher Behaviors for Productive Struggle

Now that we've looked at before, during, and after instruction, let's turn our attention to teacher behaviors. There are specific teacher behaviors that support productive struggle. As I detailed in Chapter 1, these are based on John Hattie's effect sizes. Let's look at six.

> ***Teacher Behaviors***
>
> Teacher Expectations
> Goals and Criteria
> Consideration of Prior Knowledge and Ability
> Teacher Clarity and Interpretations
> Classroom Methods and Strategies
> Scaffolding for Learning

Teacher Expectations

Teachers' beliefs, reflected in actions, demonstrate their expectations for their students. In other words, teachers treat students differently dependent on "expectancy," or what they expect. Although the difference in treatment may not be intentional, students notice it and will meet those expectations no matter how high or low they are (Williamson & Blackburn, 2016).

How do our behaviors reflect our expectations? For example, teachers tend to probe students more if they have high expectations. This sends a clear message that "I know you know the answer, and if I give you hints, you will formulate a reasonable response." Teachers also demonstrate expectations in the types of assignments or activities implemented in the classroom. Abbigail Armstrong remembered a time when her gifted students participated in thought-provoking activities such as figuring out the rise of a ramp to meet regulation to be fitted on a building, whereas her "general classes" were given drill-and-practice assignments with very little discussion of solutions and perspectives. As described by Robert Marzano (2010), let's look at typical behaviors related to low and high expectations of students.

Differential Treatment of High- and Low-Expectancy Students

	Affective Tone	Academic Content Interactions
Negative	Less eye contact Smile less Less physical contact More distance from student's seat Engage in less playful or light dialogue Use of comfort talk (That's okay, you can be good at other things) Display angry disposition	Call on less often Provide less wait time Ask less challenging questions Ask less specific questions Delve into answers less deeply Reward them for less challenging responses Provide answers for students Use simpler modes of presentation and evaluation Do not insist that homework be turned in on times Use comments such as, "Wow, I'm surprised you answered correctly" Use less praise
Positive	More eye contact Smile more More physical contact Less distance from student's seat Engage in more playful or light dialogue Little use of comfort talk (That's okay, you can be good at other things)	Call on more often Provide more wait time Ask more challenging questions Ask more specific questions Delve into answers more deeply Reward them for more challenging responses Use more complex modes of presentation and evaluation Insist that homework be turned in on time Use more praise

Marzano also provides a four-step process for identifying and addressing these differences in expectations. I've added suggestions for each step, which are helpful as you consider how to ensure overall high expectations for your students.

Marzano's Four-Step Process to Identifying Expectation Behaviors
Step 1: Identify students for whom you have low expectations.
Create a three-column chart and label each column High Expectations, Low Expectations, No Expectations. This may be a difficult task, so think of it in terms of when it comes to completing an assignment, who will turn it in early, who will turn it in on the due date with minutes to spare and who will not even bother.
Step 2: Identify similarities in students.
Consider ways your students are similar. Ask yourself, "Do I have similar expectations because of my students' similarities?" "Are my expectations high or low?" The similarities may be skin color, ethnicity, cultural group, sex or gender. This, too, is not an easy task. Discovering our own biases is challenging but if you confront why you are treating your students differently, you can begin your journey to equity in expectations.
Step 3: Identify differential treatment of low-expectancy and high-expectancy students (see chart above).
Step 4: Treat low-expectancy and high-expectancy students the same.
Choose three behaviors that you discovered you use with students for whom you have high expectations and practice these behaviors for a few days. It may be that you choose to smile at all students. It may be that if any student gives you an incorrect answer, you will give the student process time or time to ask a friend before moving on. Whatever the behavior, keep a log of the behavior and who received the treatment. Also consider technology and apps that can facilitate the change. For example, Random by ClassDojo, Transum Name Selecting App, and Random Student Selector by LiveSchool allow you to call on random students to ensure that you do not limit your choice of students for responses.

Teacher behaviors are also evidenced in the instructional tasks and assignments we ask students to complete. We'll delve into this aspect in Chapter 4, but for now, let's look at a variety of middle and high school tasks that reflect teacher behaviors. Each of the following is an example of a task or activity that reflects high expectations from teachers.

Mathematics Examples

Linear Equations

> Review the three linear equations, each of which represent a real-life situation, as well as their solutions. Determine which, if any, of the solved problems are incorrect. If there is an equation that is solved incorrectly, justify why it is incorrect, solve it correctly, and explain how you know it is now correct.

There are several characteristics of a challenging assignment reflected earlier. First, students are required to recognize and explain misconceptions, which is an aspect of reasoning as they consider the appropriateness of the solutions to the problems. Next, they must verify the reasonableness of their answers and provide a sound argument in support of their response that elaborates on the real-life situations.

Mathematical Proofs

Next, you can ask students to critique proofs, or mathematical arguments. They can critique proofs from other students or samples you provide. For example, you may provide examples of three proofs for a theorem and ask students to critique the proofs using a three-statement method.

> *Three-Statement Method*
> 1. The best proof is attempt number . . .
> 2. This is because . . .
> 3. The reason(s) the other attempts are not as strong . . .

Science Examples

> Using their knowledge of past catastrophic events that have affected the Earth and life on earth such as earthquakes, volcanic eruptions, weather devastations, and asteroid contact, students must predict the next catastrophic event that is likely to occur. They must base their prediction on research from a minimum of three sources other than the classroom text. Additionally, they must justify their prediction using their research and real-life examples and provide information as to how, if at all, people could prevent or lessen the effects of the catastrophe.

In this example, based on the range of events that happen across the world, students must make and justify a conjecture using a logical argument. Because they must research and synthesize information about past events, they are also attempting to generalize a pattern.

> Scientists are currently researching new aspects of immunobiology, with particular attention to innate immunity and adaptive immunity. Research at least three investigations related to a particular area of immunobiology. Formulate a specific research question related to immunobiology and design a new investigation that would allow you to find a solution to the question. Present your information to your group, providing a valid argument as to why your investigation would benefit society. You must cite specific evidence to support your claim.

In this project related to immunobiology, students must describe, as well as compare and contrast, methods other scientists are using to investigate immunobiology, which also provides an opportunity for students to synthesize and connect information. Students then formulate an original problem, given a situation. Finally, students are developing a logical argument while citing supporting evidence.

English/Language Arts

Reading and Writing

> Choose a controversial issue of interest to you (or from an assigned time period/political platform). Use credible sources to research the various perspectives surrounding the topic. Based on the information learned, explain two or more possible solutions to the controversy that would address the key aspects of the issue. Finally, write a logical argument that contains a proposal/compromise to satisfy groups on both sides of the conflict. In your argument, be sure to explain how you will address the problem and justify your solution with logic and evidence from research.

There are several characteristics of a challenging assignment reflected earlier. First, students are required to evaluate credibility of sources, which is an aspect of reasoning, as they consider the validity and relevance of each source. Next, they must synthesize information from numerous sources and explain possible solutions before developing a compromise that would appease all opposing viewpoints. Finally, they must use evidence from their research to justify their solution and explain how they will accomplish it.

Close Reading

> Read Malala Yousafzai's Nobel Peace Prize acceptance speech. Analyze the stylistic decisions she made when writing it. Consider her purpose, the varied syntax, connotative diction, imagery, personal testimonies, and the choice to switch from first- to second-person point of view. How do these decisions impact the overall tone and delivery of her speech?
>
> Now read the article, "In Pakistan, A Self-Styled Teacher Holds Class for 150 in a Cowshed" by Philip Reeves. How are the dreams and aspirations of Malala justified after reading about the reality of girls' education in Pakistan today? How do these differ from and compare to inequalities in American history with minority groups (African Americans, women, immigrant children)? In addition to using evidence from the texts, provide real-life examples to support your thesis.

In this example, two accessible texts are being paired, requiring a more complex level of analysis and evaluation. Not only do students need to evaluate author's craft in the first piece, they must also establish connections between the two seemingly unrelated pieces and consider how the same concept applies to other social groups in our country. This type of assignment could easily apply to any social studies reading as well.

Social Studies

Exploring Perspectives One

> #### *Dinner Parties*
>
> Imagine a dinner party with esteemed guests such as Stalin, Truman, Churchill, and Eleanor Roosevelt. Using your knowledge of the Yalta, Potsdam, and Tehran conferences in the 1940s, write a script in which these historical figures converse about their different views of what the world would look like after World War II. Choose a character and role-play this scenario, keeping the original integrity of your guest intact. At your dinner party, be sure to include what each historical figure would say about the state of society today.

In the previous example, students must take information they have learned and go beyond the knowledge gained to internalize the information and use it in another format. Students are stepping into a role-play scenario, using evidence and reasoning to generate hypothetical conversation between people with opposing viewpoints while maintaining the essence of the person's true personality. Finally, they are taking the knowledge about each of the persons and applying it to a current situation. This also requires them to move beyond the text, which in this case is what they have learned. While this assignment uses historical figures, it could easily be used with characters from a novel.

Exploring Perspectives Two

> ### *Special Interest Groups*
>
> As a class, brainstorm issues that might be taken up by special-interest groups. The list might include areas such as lessening opioid addiction, protecting animals from research, increasing school funding, etc. They will discuss what makes a special-interest group (nonprofit status, electioneering ban, etc.) and introduce sample special-interest groups and how they work.
>
> Next, students will divide into small groups, each selecting and researching a global, national, state or even local issue. Students should also research the special-interest groups that have formed around this issue, noting their size, their constituency and their messages and activities during the primaries or recent elections.
>
> Afterward, students form their own special-interest group. They must develop an agenda to promote their interest, arguments for their goals and refutations against possible opposition points. Students must include a written rationale for their position that addresses the previous points. It must include specific, factual evidence from two or three credible sources. Finally, students create a 2- to 4-minute persuasive infomercial advocating for their point of view. It should include real-life examples of how the issue affects people's lives, as well as how supporting their issue is a solution to actual problems.

In this example, students are beginning with research on special-interest groups, which in itself is not extremely challenging. However, students must extend their learning by forming their own special-interest group with a topic of choice, again researching existing special-interest groups before developing their own unique agenda with documented belief statements, arguments and refutations. All of this must be based on evidence from sources they have deemed credible. The assignment culminates with a persuasive campaign to advocate for their interest. This idea of making research become more relevant and personal helps students to dig deeper, make more connections and use reasoning skills that wouldn't have happened with a simple research paper on special-interest groups. This could be easily adapted for an ELA classroom at any grade level by focusing on the research skills and argumentative writing standards.

> **Middle/High School Art Example**
>
> *Critiquing Art*
>
> Students move through an art gallery of work created by their classmates. Each student chooses one piece of art and writes a short critique. The critique must include the student's opinion of the artwork, support of the opinion based on the lesson taught by the teacher and the student's own experiences, and recommendations for improvement.

In the art example, students are evaluating a sample piece of art. However, they must justify their opinion and recommendation based on what they have been taught and their own experiences in art, requiring students to push beyond surface information.

> **Sculpture**
>
> *Mini-Gallery*
>
> Using Google Arts and Culture as a database, create a mini-gallery of five sculptures, built around a common theme. In a program for the gallery, describe how the thematic mini-gallery reflects the elements and principles of Sculpture, which includes a short rationale for your selection.

In the Sculpture sample, students must create a gallery. However, by requiring them to follow and justify a theme for the gallery, they will experience productive struggle.

> **Chorus/Band/Drama/Theatre**
>
> *Critiquing a Performance*
>
> Students listens/views a performance of your choice (either their own or one on the internet). Each student writes a short critique, which must include the student's opinion of the work, support of the opinion based on the lessons taught by the teacher and the student's own experiences, and recommendations for improvement.

Similar to the art evaluation, students in classes that utilize performances can ask students to go beyond giving their opinion to critiquing a performance using what they have learned and experienced.

Graphic Design

Design a Marketing Campaign

You've been hired by a company (you can choose the type, such as clothing, computer game, phone, etc.). First, write a paragraph describing the company and their goals. Next, they have asked you to create a portfolio of three graphic design items, such as a screenshot, poster, logo, etc. It must incorporate all elements of graphic design that you have learned in class in a persuasive manner, and it must appeal to the audience for the item. You'll also write a reflection justifying your choices.

Through graphic design, students move beyond basic application to persuading an audience. They also justify their choices based on their learning.

Technology

Data Tracking: Dangers and Benefits

Building on our class discussion, find at least three credible sources on the topic of data tracking. In particular, you are looking at both the advantages and disadvantages of using data tracking. Design a tool (video, webpage, etc.) designed to convince your audience of your perspective on data tracking. For example, if you believe companies should be allowed to use data tracking, create a technology-based format to convince others of your belief. In your information, you should include the reasons that support your position, as well as addressing the typical objections.

By creating a technology-based tool to convince an audience of their perspective on data tracking, students are required to find information to justify their perspective as well as evaluating the other perspective. This requires them to push through the standard information to fully understand the issue.

Junior ROTC

Warning Order

Prepare to move out in ten minutes with a full battle load and materials necessary to cross a 30 meter stream and resupply the only heavy weapon remaining on site; a 50 cal. A Special Forces Team has been engaging a mid-sized force of dedicated ISIS outside the town of Farraht. Farraht is located on a hilltop 2K to the east of your position over a rapid and deep stream. The fight has been for the valley below the village. The team took significant casualties and has withdrawn. One SF soldier remained behind to cover the withdrawal. The AC130 gunship can only remain on station for 45 minutes before they are bingo for fuel. At that time the position is expected to be overrun by a superior force. A drone is in place and will monitor the situation. It has only one Hellfire missile to defend your withdrawal. Once you reach the stream use normal comms to have it release on the final vehicle to destroy sensitive materials and communication equipment. If the drone detects the vehicle is being overrun it will fire on the vehicle even if you are in proximity. After the 45 minute estimate from now one F117 will drop ordinance on the valley destroying everyone who remains. We move out in 10 minutes!

Consider this your OP order. Construct a one rope bridge. Each person in your squad needs to carry a can 50 caliber ammunition across the bridge to resupply and man the remaining vehicle. You must maintain security on both sides of the river so long as two soldiers remain on that side. When only one soldier remains, he or she may cross the river in the manner necessary to take down the bridge. After your final crossing you must disassemble the bridge to leave no trace of your activities on either side leaving the enemy without further intelligence of our tactics and methods.

Students productively struggle with this Junior ROTC activity that requires strong problem-solving skills, including analysis and evaluation.

Goals and Criteria

As you plan your lessons, it's important to have clear learning goals and criteria that are appropriately challenging (Chapter 4). One strategy I like is the concept of SMART goals.

SMART	
S	Specific
M	Measurable
A	Attainable
R	Realistic
T	Timely

One mistake I often see is that teachers use standards or objectives from another source. For example, I saw the following objective: Students will realize how living things adapt to their environment. What does it mean to realize something? How will students demonstrate understanding? Do they already know information about living things? Here's a SMART version of the same objective.

By the end of the unit, students will be able to identify at least three specific ways that animals adapt survive in their environment and accurately explain how each adaptation supports survival, as measured by a writing assessment with 80% accuracy.

Additionally, students must understand the criteria for success. You'll want to plan for this from the start of your planning. Do you want them to be able to answer a specific question? Do you want them to write an essay with three key points and evidence for each point? Be sure they know how they should show what they know. I've found rubrics are particularly helpful—they help me clarify what I'm looking for and they help students understand what I think "good looks like."

Science Project Rubric			
	Exemplary	*Acceptable*	*Not Yet (Do Over)*
Problem and Hypothesis	• Problem is new meaningful, well researched. • Hypothesis is clearly stated in the "IF . . . THEN" format.	• Problem is meaningful and researched. • Hypothesis is stated.	• Problem is addressed vaguely with little research support. • Hypothesis is unclear or not stated.

	Science Project Rubric		
	Exemplary	*Acceptable*	*Not Yet (Do Over)*
Research Support	• Research is thorough, specific, and includes many examples. • All ideas are clearly explained. • History, biology, and pros and cons are fully addressed.	• Research has some specifics and examples. • Most ideas are explained. • Student mostly addresses the history, biology, and pros and cons.	• Research has little specifics and few examples. • Two or fewer ideas are explained. • Student doesn't address all or any areas: history, biology, and pros and cons.
Variables	• Variables have been identified, controls are appropriate, in place, and explained. • Sample size is appropriate and explained.	• Variables have been somewhat identified, controls are appropriate and in place. • Sample size appropriate.	• Missing variables or controls. • Sample size is not appropriate or is not considered.

Consideration of Prior Knowledge and Ability

Third, teachers who encourage productive struggle consider prior knowledge and ability when planning lessons. Yes, you want to provide challenging tasks, but you don't want to ignore your students' readiness to learn. We'll look at multiple ways to assess prior knowledge in Chapter 5 (Scaffolding), but here let's look readiness.

Readiness

The heart of teaching is to take a student from where he or she is, and move him or her to a higher level of learning. To do that, you need to understand where a student is in terms of knowledge and understanding. Ideally, you assess readiness levels before you start units or lessons, and you continue to assess changing readiness levels using formative assessments.

Pre-Tests

I've known teachers who use a pre-test for the year, using a broad range of questions to identify topics that might need less instruction. A far more effective approach in my experience, is to use pre-testing to measure students' understanding of key topics, which usually means a learning unit, such as a two-week study of landforms.

Characteristics of Effective Pre-Tests

Focused on essential skills

Incorporates questions that determine if they understand necessary background knowledge

Incorporates questions that determine if they understand concepts planned for instruction

Incorporates questions that determine if they have advanced knowledge of concepts

Is not overwhelming for students

Questions are clear and understandable

Observations

An important formative assessment tool for teachers is the use of observations. Observations can be planned, or they can be spontaneous. In an observation, you simply observe what students are doing, and take notes for documentation. You may choose to observe for particular instructional behaviors, or you may simply observe to see what happens from a general standpoint. Checklists, which provide a quick way for you to make notes about your observations can be simple yes/no tallies, or they can be open-ended for teachers to add notes.

> **Sample Band Checklist**
>
> ____Maintains correct posture and playing position
> ____Follows conductor attentively (eye contact, starts/stops on cue)
> ____Plays with appropriate tone, rhythm, and dynamics
> ____Demonstrates respectful rehearsal behavior (no talking out of turn, handles instrument responsibly)

Interviews and Conferences

In interviews and conferences, the teacher meets with students to assess understanding of content. For either of these, the teacher plans a series of questions to ask a student about his or her learning. It's also important to stay flexible and adjust questions during the interview or conference. These are probably used most often in writing situations, but they can be used with any subject area.

> **Sample Writing Conference Questions**
>
> Please tell me a little about your writing.
> What do you think is going well?
> Show me an example of that.
> What are you struggling with?
> Show me an example.
> How do you think you can improve on your own?
> How can I help you?
> What are your next steps?

Teacher Clarity and Interpretations

Another evidence-based key to effective instruction, especially in the productive struggle classroom, is related to teacher clarity and interpretations. There are three aspects in this area.

> Teacher clarity.
> Organization of instruction.
> Interpretations based on assessment of student learning.

As we consider clarity, I remember a situation when I was a teacher. I had explained something to my students, but they didn't understand. I explained again, but they were still confused. One of my students said, "Can you just tell us what's in your head?" That clicked with me. I just assumed they knew certain concepts, but they didn't. I decided to "think like a beginner" and taught the lesson again, this time successfully. When I clarified my instruction, the students were successful.

Also, your instruction should be organized in a way to maximize learning. This includes activating prior knowledge, connecting to other learning, and providing options for applying learning to real life. You can also use the 5E method, which was developed by Roger Bybee and his colleagues.

> Engage
> Explore
> Explain
> Elaborate
> Evaluate

A final aspect of this category is that effective teachers make interpretations based on assessment of student learning. In other words, as you incorporate formative assessment throughout your lesson, you actually use that information to make instructional adjustments. We'll talk more about this in Chapter 6.

Classroom Methods and Strategies

There are a variety of classroom strategies and methods that are particularly effective in the productive struggle classroom. Although we won't go into detail on each at this time, notice that in all of the options listed later, there is a high level of student involvement and student ownership and a shift in the teacher's role to facilitator.

> Small Group
> Class Discussion
> Inquiry-Based Teaching
> Constructivist Teaching
> Inductive Teaching
> Cognitive Task Analysis
> Problem-Solving Teaching
> Teaching Students to Drive Their Learning
> Self-regulation Learning

Scaffolding for Learning

Finally, teachers who encourage productive struggle provide scaffolding, including giving examples and offering guided practice. Chapter 5 focuses specifically on these incorporating these areas, but for now, let's look at a rubric overview.

Rubric for Teacher Behaviors

	Beginning	Emerging	Accomplished
Teacher Expectations	Expectations are based on preconceived and perhaps outdated notions of what students should be able to do. Expectations differ based on the identified label of each student (special needs, honors, etc.).	Expectations are built on what students are currently able to do, with some ideas about raising the level of challenge. There is an acknowledgement that teachers play a role in helping students meet high expectations. There are also high expectations for advanced and/or gifted students.	Expectations are balanced between what students can currently do, but what they have the potential to do. High expectations incorporate that part of the teacher's role is to scaffold students for success.
Goals and Criteria	Goals are general; criteria is somewhat clear.	Goals are specific, with general criteria for students.	SMART goals provide very clear criteria for success.

	Beginning	*Emerging*	*Accomplished*
	\multicolumn{3}{c}{***Rubric for Teacher Behaviors***}
Consideration of Prior Knowledge and Ability	There is minimal understanding of students' prior knowledges and abilities based on existing information. The understanding is minimally reflected in lesson planning and implementation.	There is some understanding of students' prior knowledges and abilities based on some assessments. The understanding is reflected in lesson planning and implementation.	A detailed understanding of prior knowledge and ability is built on multiple sources and is thoroughly integrated into lesson planning and implementation.
Teacher Clarity and Interpretations	Teacher provides lessons that are sometimes clear and detailed, somewhat organized, and may or may not reflect interpretations of assessment of student learning.	Teacher provides lessons that are clear, somewhat detailed, organized, and somewhat reflect interpretations of assessment of student learning.	Teacher provides lessons that are clear, detailed, extremely organized, and thoroughly reflect interpretations of assessment of student learning.

(Continued)

Rubric for Teacher Behaviors			
	Beginning	*Emerging*	*Accomplished*
Classroom Strategies and Methods	Teacher either minimally uses or does not use evidence-based strategies and methods that are conducive to productive struggle.	Teacher uses some evidence-based strategies and methods that are conducive to productive struggle.	Teacher incorporates evidence-based strategies and methods that are conducive to productive struggle.
Scaffolding for Learning	Teacher uses scaffolding, generally for all students that supports the productive struggle classroom.	Teacher sometimes incorporates scaffolding for all students that supports the productive struggle classroom. He or she attempts to individual scaffolding.	Teacher thoroughly incorporates scaffolding, both general and individualized, that supports the productive struggle classroom.

Student Behaviors

Now let's turn our attention from teacher behaviors to student behaviors, such as students' self-expectations, self-regulation, metacognitive reflection, and learning together.

Expectations

Just as teachers' expectations matter, so do students' expectations. A student's expectations of himself or herself drive much of what happens with learning. How can we help build students' expectations? We discussed this in Chapter 2, but as a brief recap, here are some strategies.

> Believe each student has unlimited potential.
> Encourage them whenever they make a mistake.
> Support students to ensure growth.
> Create a growth mindset.
> Challenge them in learning activities.

Self-Regulation

Self-regulation for students involves several areas: effort, concentration, persistence, and engagement.

We want students to show effort and persistence because it positively impacts student learning. Encouraging and reinforcing effort are particularly critical for those students who do not understand the importance of their own efforts. In *Classroom Instruction that Works*, Marzano et al. (2001) make two important comments regarding students' views about effort.

> ### *Research-Based Generalizations About Effort*
> - Not all students realize the importance of believing in effort.
> - Students can learn to change their beliefs to an emphasis on effort.
>
> (Marzano et al., 2001, p. 50)

This is positive news for teachers. First, we're not imagining it—students don't realize they need to exert effort. And second, we can help them change that belief. Richard Curwin describes seven specific ways to encourage effort.

7 Ways to Encourage Effort

1. Never fail a student who tries, and never give the highest grades to one who doesn't.
2. Start with the positive.
3. See mistakes as learning opportunities, not failures.
4. Give do overs.
5. Give students the test before you start a unit.
6. Limit your corrections.
7. Do not compare students.

We also want students to show concentration and engagement. When they are involved in learning, they typically concentrate of the activity, becoming highly engaged. This happens when they are intrinsically motivated (Chapter 2), and when we create opportunities for them to be engaged. Productive struggle is an ideal activity for concentration and engagement, especially if designed well. We'll look more at this in Chapter 4, where we explore how to pick the right tasks and activities.

Metacognitive Reflection

Another key for your students is their metacognitive reflection. There are five types of metacognitive reflection.

> Evaluation and reflection
> Strategy monitoring
> Self-judgement and reflection
> Metacognitive strategies
> Self-verbalization and self-questioning

Students don't learn these strategies on their own; we need to model them, teach them, and allow them to practice them. We'll look at how to do that in Chapter 5 (Scaffolding).

Learning Together

Students in a productive struggle classroom also learn together. Even when they are working individually, they reach out to each other for feedback. There are five ways students learn together.

> Questioning
> Elaborative interrogation
> Collaborative learning
> Reciprocal teaching
> Classroom discussion

There are specific strategies that support each of these five options. We'll discuss them in Chapter 5.

> ***Self-Scaffolding Strategies***
>
> Organizing and transforming notes
> Study skills
> Concept mapping
> Graphic organizers and concept maps
> Elaboration and organization

Now, let's look at a rubric to assess student behaviors.

Rubric for Student Behaviors			
	Beginning	*Emerging*	*Accomplished*
Student Expectations	Teacher attempts to model high expectations for students, believes that some students can learn at high levels, and tries to help some students develop a growth mindset. A few students have high expectations for themselves.	Teacher sometimes models high expectations for students, believes that some students can learn at high levels, and helps all students develop a growth mindset. This results in some students having high expectations for themselves.	Teacher models high expectations for students, believes that each student can learn at high levels, encourages and supports those high expectations, and helps all students develop a growth mindset. This results in all students having high expectations for themselves.
Self-Regulation	Some students demonstrate effort, concentration, persistence, and engagement, but the majority do not.	Students sometimes demonstrate effort, concentration, persistence, and engagement.	Students consistently demonstrate high levels of effort, concentration, persistence, and engagement.

	Rubric for Student Behaviors		
	Beginning	*Emerging*	*Accomplished*
Metacognitive Reflection	Teacher may teach students a metacognitive strategy. Students may or may not use the strategy during productive struggle.	Teacher teaches students some metacognitive strategies and gives opportunities for practice. Students sometimes use metacognitive strategies during productive struggle.	Teacher teaches students a variety of strategies for metacognitive reflection, models their use, and gives opportunities for guided and independent practice. Students utilize the metacognitive strategies appropriately during productive struggle.
Learning Together	Teacher provides some activities for students to learn together. Students attempt to work together to complete a task.	Teacher provides a variety of structured activities for students to learn together. Students collaborate at some level to help each other learn.	Teacher provides a variety of well-designed, structured activities for students to learn together. Students collaborate at high levels to help each other learn.

(Continued)

Rubric for Student Behaviors

	Beginning	Emerging	Accomplished
Self-Scaffolding Strategies	Teacher may teach students a self-scaffolding strategy. Students may or may not use the strategy during productive struggle.	Teacher teaches students some self-scaffolding strategies and gives opportunities for practice. Students sometimes use self-scaffolding strategies during productive struggle.	Teacher teaches students a variety of self-scaffolding strategies, models their use, and gives opportunities for guided and independent practice. Students utilize the self-scaffolding strategies appropriately during productive struggle.

A Final Note

To build a productive struggle classroom, teachers need to build a climate and teach students how to successfully participate in productive struggle. Then, it's important to provide instruction that supports productive struggle before, during, and after the task. Finally, you'll want to incorporate the teacher and student behaviors that support productive instruction.

Points to Ponder

1. What can you do to improve your climate so it will support productive struggle?
2. Which of the before-during-after strategies do you want to try?
3. What teacher behaviors do you exhibit? Are there ways to improve?
4. What student behaviors would you like to encourage?

Continue the Learning

Use the QR Code to access videos for your own use or for group professional development.

4

What Is the Right Level for Productive Struggle?

One of the key concerns with productive struggle is how to determine the right level of the task or material. In other words, how do I know if something is too hard, too easy, or just right? In this chapter, we'll look at five areas that can help us make that determination.

> Vygotsky's Zone of Proximal Development
> Flow from Mihaly Csikszentmihalyi
> Determining Appropriately Leveled Text Materials
> Appropriately Challenging Skills and Tasks
> What Is the Difference Between An Explanation and a Justification?

Vygotsky's Zone of Proximal Development

In 1978, Lev Vygotsky theorized that there is a zone of proximal development (ZPD) for learners. He posits that students sometimes do work that is too easy or is in their comfort zone. Other times, they work at a level that is too challenging therefore, they are in a frustration level. In the zone of proximal development, students are working at the ideal learning level. Students may need help, or they may have to persist to be successful, but this is where they learn best.

He provides more detail:

> The distance between the actual developmental level (of the learner) as determined by independent problem solving and the level of potential development as determined through problem solving under adult guidance, or in collaboration with more capable peers.
> (Vygotsky, 1978, p. 86)

Let's review his words: we are looking at the distance between the actual developmental level and the potential developmental level. That's the area of potential growth, and it's exactly the sweet spot for productive struggle. Determining the ZPD comes from assessment, which we'll speak to in Chapter 6. However, he also notes that adult guidance or collaboration is needed. In other words, scaffolding, which we'll address in Chapter 5, is critical.

> ***Critical Components of the Zone of Proximal Development***
>
> Assessment to Determine Current Developmental Level
> Vision of Potential Developmental Level
> Guidance and Collaboration
> Scaffolding

These components provide key structural components for teachers to help meet students' needs.

Flow From Mihaly Csikszentmihalyi

In 1975, psychologist Mihaly Csiksentmihalyi introduced the concept of flow, which is a mental state that occurs when a person is completely immersed in a task or activity. There are several characteristics of flow.

> Complete concentration
> A full understanding of what to do
> Intrinsic motivation
> Appropriately challenging level of skill

As with Vygotsky's Zone of Proximal Development, students are working at a level that provides challenge—just not too much. Csikszentmihalyi describes that level as occurring when "one's skills are adequate to cope with the challenges at hand, in a goal-directed, rule-bound action system that provides clear clues as to how one is performing" (2009). For teachers, this implies that we need to equip students (Chapter 5) with skills, such as problem-solving, that allow them to meet the challenge, and we need to provide structure (Chapter 3) to help them be successful.

Determining Appropriately Leveled Text Materials

Oftentimes, because we want student to be successful, we move them into materials that are in their comfort zone. One of the major areas for productive struggle is through the texts used during teaching. It's important for students to read a book or an article they can quickly and easily finish; those opportunities build self-confidence, provide enjoyable experiences, increase fluency and may increase student motivation. But if that's all students read, they never learn how to deal with more challenging materials. We should consider providing text materials in all subject areas that are in a student's zone of proximal development.

I'd like to take a moment and add a cautionary note to our discussion. The concept of leveled texts can be controversial, mainly because they have been misused at times. For example, I visited a school where every book was labeled with a number and students were never allowed to read a book that was not in their identified range. I spoke to a student who wanted to read a higher-level book, and he was very motivated by the topic. However, the teacher told him no because of the number. That's not best practice with leveling. A student who is highly motivated by the topic can often push through and read a more challenging book. Leveled text is a guide, not a limitation. Another example is with a struggling student who doesn't have much confidence in himself. In that case, I may want to help him choose an easier book to build fluency and confidence, in order to then move back up to something more challenging. And there are some books that may have a lower score on a readability scale, but the content is more difficult, perhaps due to the concepts described or the use of figurative language. Using leveled text is more of an art than a science, and it's critical that you use your judgment as a part of the process.

Now, what are the positive reasons to use leveled text? The authors of *Beyond Leveled Text* (2nd edition) describe seven aspects of leveling books for readers.

> Readers make the most progress when books are not too easy or too difficult.
>
> Considering a just-right level helps readers read fluently and comprehend better; thus they take of the traits and skills of better readers.
>
> Students who meet success in reading are more likely to persist, to read more with less off-task behavior, and to achieve more.
>
> Acceleration in learning, or increased achievement, is possible for struggling readers when the text/reading level is match.
>
> Groups of books into levels can make it easier to teachers, parents, and children to select books to read.
>
> Books that are used for instruction can be selected with emphasis on student needs at a certain point, but selections should be different for independent reading.
>
> With the variety of books available with leveling features, schools can adapt a greater number of their book collections to support their particular students.

Look for a balance: Material should be difficult enough that students are learning something new, but not so hard that they give up. If you like to play tennis, you'll improve if you play against someone who is better than you. But if you play against Venus and Serena Williams, you'll learn less because you are overwhelmed by their advanced skill level. A good guideline is that for text to be appropriately challenging for growth, students should be able to understand about 75% of what they read. That percentage means students understand the majority of the material, while learning something new. One option for increasing text difficulty is to identify where your students are reading and provide text materials that match their level of growth.

When I was teaching, I used books that were labeled on grade level, but in reality, they were much easier than what students were expected to read on the state test or in real-life materials. That is still true today, and that is why it is important to use a measure that is consistent across all texts. There are a variety of readability formulas, which provide standard for text difficulty you can use to select texts.

Popular Readability Formulas	
Fry	The most widely used of the readability formulas. The Fry is based on the assumption that the longer the sentence and the longer the word, the more difficult the passage.
Flesch-Kincaid	The Flesch-Kincaid is embedded in Microsoft Word programs and checks documents for the reading level of the passage.
Fountas and Pinnell Benchmark Assessment System	There are 26 levels in the Fountas and Pinnell System
The Lexile Framework	The Lexile Framework is a computerized formula that analyzes entire text selections by sentence length and word frequency. It allows you to link difficulty of text materials with standardized tests. The web site provides a searchable database of books, and many national and state tests also provide Lexile levels for students based on test scores.

No matter which tool you use to determine the difficulty of text materials, remember that text difficulty is only one factor to consider when selecting text for or with your students. Other considerations include the appropriateness of the text for the students' age or developmental levels, the content of the material, and the purpose for reading, such as for interest or research.

> **Considerations for Text Selection**
>
> Is the content of the text pertinent to my standards or objectives?
>
> Is the content of the text appropriate to the purpose of the assignment (independent reading, research, partner reading, etc.)?
>
> Is the content of the text appropriate to the age or developmental level of my students?
>
> Is the content of the text appropriately challenging for growth (not too hard, yet not too easy)?
>
> Is this the only opportunity my students will be given to read, or are they allowed choices at other times?

Remember to always use your professional judgment when selecting text materials for your struggling students. Any readability formula may be the starting point for book selection, but it should never be the only factor considered. The goal is always to pick the right resource for the right reader at the right time. Remember to think about all aspects of the book or text and preview materials to ensure they are appropriate for your students.

Students' Determination of Reading Level

You may have situations where you want students to self-determine if a book is appropriately challenging. Here's a simple three level rubric students can use to choose a leveled text. Note that my levels equate appropriately challenging with productive struggle—they are more challenging than some other rules in existence, such as the Goldilocks Rules.

Choose a book or article you would like to read. Read it to yourself and count the number of words you don't know or understand. Choose the column with the number of words.		
0-2 Words	3-6	7 or More
Very Easy	Appropriately Challenging	Too Hard

Ultimately, what you want to do is balance the level of materials for your students. Too often, we lower the level of text for our struggling students, especially in the content areas such as science and social studies. A part of high expectations is providing text that is challenging for students, then balancing that challenge by providing the appropriate support and scaffolding so students can be successful.

Appropriately Challenging Skills and Tasks

Finally, we'll turn our attention to appropriately challenging skills and tasks. How do we determine what is appropriately challenging? As we've discussed earlier in this chapter, you'll want to use your judgment in making final decisions, but I wanted to give you a guide that describes key skills and tasks that are challenging. This is built on national frameworks such as Depth of Knowledge and the Cognitive Rigor Matrix, as well as my extensive work for over 20 years on rigor. You may find that you need to start with the chart for Developing Skills, but I'd encourage you to move to the set of Appropriately Challenging Criteria. Your students may struggle, but that's the point!

There are many skills we assume are challenging to students, but they actually aren't. It's important to recognize that these skills may develop the skills needed for challenging work, but they aren't what we are looking at for productive struggle.

Developing Skills

Apply

Summarize

Interpret

Predict

Infer

Compare and contrast

Relevant/irrelevant information

Explaining

Locating information

Developing hypotheses

Select math procedure according to criteria

Create diagram or model to demonstrate understanding

I understand you may be thinking that, for some of your students, especially struggling students, the developing tasks are challenging. When students haven't been working at challenging levels, then these tasks are difficult. But that shouldn't be the goal. Each of these tasks should be considered building blocks—something that is a stepping stone to truly challenging work. They may even be part of a student task, one that is a precursor for appropriately challenging work.

So what types of tasks and activities are considered challenging?

> **Appropriately Challenging Work for Productive Struggle**
>
> Identifying and explaining misconceptions (error analysis)
> Proposing and evaluating solutions
> Justifications, going beyond the text
> Defending with evidence
> Open-ended situations
> Synthesizing
> Generalizing
> Reframing ideas
> Grappling with complex text
> Identifying questions and designing investigations
> Designing mathematical models
> Analyzing how changes have affected people and places
> Developing alternate solutions
> Developing a logical argument for concepts

Let's look at sample productive struggle tasks that reflect these appropriately challenging criteria. You'll notice how many are open ended, which provides an excellent opportunity for productive struggle.

> **Middle School Math**
>
> *Three-Statement Method*
> 1. The best solution is attempt number . . .
> 2. This is because . . .
> 3. The reason(s) the other attempts are not as strong . . .

In this case, students review three solutions. They determine which one is the best solution and justify their response. Then, they must document why the other attempts are not as strong.

High School Math

Pythagorean Theorem . . . What Is That?

Thanks to Pythagoras, we have a great equation that we can use to find the length of the sides of a right triangle. The theorem is used in architecture, navigation and surveying, which are important parts of our lives, but what if Pythagoras had never come up with the theorem? Sure, you could use measurement of a tool, but some things may be impossible to measure such as if you are trying to find distances between long navigation points. For instance, a plane can use its height above the ground and its distance from the destination airport to find the correct place to begin a descent to that airport. It seems like something is left out. Your charge is to come up with a replacement equation that would assist you with the following problem. You should be able to explain how you came up with the new equation and also include the drawbacks of using this equation. Pythagoras can't be replaced, but I bet you can come close.

Your grandmother is moving in with you and needs wheel access to your home. The height of your current porch steps are 4.5ft. Your dad said that he thinks the ramp needs to be 10ft long. Based on your dad's guess, would you be able to build the ramp to meet these specifications? Explain how you came up with a new equation instead of Pythagorean Theorem to solve this equation. Include the drawbacks of using this equation.

https://sciencing.com/real-life-uses-pythagorean-theorem-8247514.html

---

Here, students are given a situation, and struggle to develop a new solution, one that is an alternative to the Pythagorean Theorem. Depending on the complexity of the situation, you might adapt this so that students are formulating a mathematical model.

> **Middle School Science**
>
> Design an investigation to test the effects of temperature on how enzymes break down food with limited materials.

For middle school science, students are required to design their own investigation, which requires them to evaluate the issue and determine what will provide an answer to the research question.

> **High School Science**
>
> You are a scientist researching new vaccines to combat viruses in our society. Research the benefits and disadvantages on all stakeholders, including analyzing biases that exist. Then, create a proposed set of vaccine development guidelines to send to the CDC that are justified by scientific evidence rather than opinion.

For this example, students must not only research the topic, they must look for biases by specific researchers. After identifying key scientific facts, they struggle to create and justify a set of guidelines.

> **Middle School Social Studies**
>
> Analyze two historical primary sources that provide information about the same historical event. Explore biases and determine which of the two is a more reliable source, justifying their choice with evidence.

Similar to the high school science example, students must complete research and explore the biases that exist. Based on that, they determine the more reliable source and provide evidence for their choice.

> **High School Social Studies**
>
> Students divide into small groups, each selecting and researching a global, national, state or even local issue. Students should also research the special-interest groups that have formed around this issue, noting their size, their constituency and their messages and activities during the primaries or recent elections.
>
> Afterward, students form their own special-interest group. They must develop an agenda to promote their interest, arguments for their goals and refutations against possible opposition points. Students must include a written rationale for their position that addresses the previous points. It must include specific, factual evidence from two or three credible sources. Finally, students create a 2- to 4-minute persuasive infomercial advocating for their point of view. It should include real-life examples of how the issue affects people's lives, as well as how supporting their issue is a solution to actual problems.

After researching a key issue and the related special interest groups, students form their own special interest group. They must thoroughly analyze the issues around the group, develop and agenda, and create arguments that will refute the opposition. Additionally, they must go beyond their core research to apply their issue to real life.

> **Middle School English/Language Arts**
>
> What is the theme of *Goldilocks and the Three Bears*? Use details from the text to support your choice. It was written nearly 200 years ago. Justify whether this theme applies to today. Provide an example from modern life to validate your answer

Middle school students analyze the theme of *Goldilocks and the Three Bears* and provide justification as to its applicability to our current life.

High School English/Language Arts

We have been reading dystopian novels. You have been given the opportunity to start a new society on a deserted island that is fully equipped with all needed amenities and modern technology. The island is not owned or under the influence of any nation. It is the responsibility of your group to inhabit the island in any manner that you choose. By completing the following assignments and working cooperatively, your group will build the perfect society and will introduce your society to the class.

- Note characteristics of healthy societies and governments (past and present) through online research.
- Note the pitfalls of unhealthy societies and governments (past and present) through online research.
- Determine the criteria you think would make the perfect society (type of government, freedoms, laws, technology available, etc.).
- Create a multimedia campaign advertising your community to the rest of the world. Use persuasive appeals, but justify your choices with evidence from research you conducted and the books we have read in book clubs.

In this particular example, students have just completed reading various dystopian novels in a book club format. In mixed groups, they will share what worked or didn't work in the book they read before researching societies and governments from the past and present together. The goal here is to discern the qualities that allow a society to thrive versus those that seem to indicate flaws in infrastructure of the government. Afterward, they will self-select qualities and norms from the various governments researched to establish the criteria for a perfect society from their perspective. Students will use research-based evidence to produce a campaign using various forms of media (i.e. short video, blog, visual advertisement, interview, audio, etc.) that will attract people to their community.

Foreign Language

Translate a short story that includes idioms that do not have direct equivalents.

In a creative twist, the sample story provided for translation includes information that does not have a direct translation. Students will need to use their depth of knowledge of the language to struggle to paraphrase the idioms.

> ### *Technology*
>
> Your school newspaper wants to feature a series of articles about student life. You are part of a data mining team tasked with finding trends such as study habits, sleep, extracurricular activities, and social media use that might inform how schools should support students. Identify how you will collect data, how you will identify trends, and then do an investigation for the articles.

In a technology class, this focus on data mining requires students to analyze trends, evaluate data that supports the trends, and use the data to justify conclusions in the investigation.

> ### *Art*
>
> Students move through an art gallery of work created by their classmates. Each student chooses one piece of art and writes a short critique. The critique must include the student's opinion of the artwork, support of the opinion based on the lesson taught by the teacher and the student's own experiences, and recommendations for improvement.

The art sample requires students to evaluate a piece of art and critique it based on their learning and their own experiences, rather than simply providing their opinion with examples.

> ### *Chorus*
>
> Groups are provided a piece with unexpected harmonies and other notes for them to master.

After students have achieved a basic level of mastery, they are required to sing a piece with unpredictable harmonies and notes, necessitating creative application of their skills.

> ### *Band*
>
> Provide a piece of music with missing measures, rests, or intentionally altered rhythms. Students must "fill in the gaps" by predicting or composing what belongs, testing their understanding of harmony, rhythm, and style.

When students are given music with missing information, students must struggle to find the "right" answer (there is typically more than one right answer), so they must make and defend musical choices.

> ### *Physical Education*
>
> Develop a series of tests to measure a student's fitness level. After you receive the results, interpret the results and develop a long-term fitness plan for the student.

In physical education, students can productively struggle to design a series of tests, review and interpret results, and develop a long-term plan.

> ### *Theatre Arts*
>
> In small groups, create a playbill to show that you understand all the components that go into a production. You'll also get a taste for marketing. Be sure you include costume descriptions, set descriptions, plot summary, fake cast and crew lists, and an evocative cover design. Also, write a paper justifying your choices and the impact you hope it would make on your audience.

In addition to analyzing production components, students must struggle to justify their choices and the possible impact of the playbill.

Career and Technical Education

You are the owner of a business that recycles computer equipment. Your driving purpose is: "How can we utilize older computer equipment in economical, business-connected ways?"

Create a business plan that addresses how to re-use older equipment in an economical, business-connected way. Include if there is some equipment that should just be disposed of, the impacts to the business community and environment of disposal, the costs of re-utilizing old equipment, and the benefits and disadvantages of re-using older equipment in an economical, business-connected way. Be specific as to how you would re-use the equipment so that it meets the criteria.

In addition to applying key information about computers, students must analyze the implication of their choices and evaluate appropriate uses for older technology.

Family and Consumer Sciences

Develop a healthy eating plan for a family of three on a fixed budget (determined in advance). It's also important that one of the three family members is a diabetic. The healthy plan should include nutritious and tasty choices for all members.

Students can participate in productive struggle by developing a healthy eating plan given several key parameters.

> ### *Agricultural Education*
> Given a small plot of land, plan a crop rotation, balancing all related considerations including balancing soil health, yield, and potential setbacks. Justify your choices.

For agricultural education, students must evaluate information to plan a crop rotation, then justify your choices to show you made the best decision.

> ### *Media/Journalism*
> After researching two media sources that have different perspectives, analyze which of the two is more credible. Justify your decision with evidence from the sources, at least one more source, and your own experiences.

This assignment focuses on issues of bias and credibility, with an additional emphasis on justification.

> ### *Debate/Speech*
> Choose a side for a debate. Then, participate in a debate in which you argue the other side.

Once students choose a side on an issue, they must research and debate the opposing side. Requiring students to argue the "other" side, they are forced to evaluate the issue at a higher level.

Engineering/Makerspace

Objective

Working in teams of two, design and build a bridge using balsa wood to hold as much weight as possible over a span of 30 cm while using the least amount of material.

Constraints

1. The overall width of the bridge must be at least 7 cm and may not exceed 10 cm.
2. The overall length of the bridge must be at least 33 cm long and may not exceed 35 cm.
3. The overall height of the bridge must be at least 7 cm and may not exceed 35 cm.
4. A block (8 cm long, 5 cm wide, 1.9 cm thick) must be able to pass through the bridge. Think of this as a car. This block will be used for applying a load to your bridge.
5. The bridge shall allow a 3/8-inch bolt to pass through the center of the bridge deck. This will be used for applying a load to your bridge.
6. Glue may only be used at the joints of the wood members.
7. Wood joints may be notched if desired.
8. If gussets made from card stock are used, they must be used on both sides of a joint in order to reinforce and strengthen the joint.
9. Lamanation of balsa wood members is not permitted.
10. Bridge cross members may not be closer than 2 cm to each other.

Write a reflection justifying why your bridge construction is the best model, using what you have learned in class and from your construction, and explain the practical uses of your bridge.

Finally, students productively struggle in this assignment where they must not only build an effective bridge, they must also justify their choices. Each of these examples provides a picture of productive struggle.

What Is the Difference Between an Explanation and a Justification?

A key difference in work that requires productive struggle is explanation vs. justification. Too often, we ask students to explain a statement or explain why they think something is true. When you explain something, you are simply giving your opinion, although you may give an example. It's perfectly appropriate, but usually does not require productive struggle to produce it. On the other hand, when you justify something, you state an argument and base your thoughts or analysis on specific evidence from the text or lesson. You link that evidence to your comment or analysis. The next natural step is to go beyond the text into other learning or real life. Let's look at some samples that show the difference.

Explanation vs. Justification	
Explanation	*Justification*
Why is X the main character?	Justify your choice of main character using specific actions he or she takes and how those actions reflect a main character rather than a supporting character.
Which novel do you like better and why?	Explain your choice using specific examples from the text and why it links to your life (be specific).
How did you solve the problem?	Justify your answer using what you have learned in class and using math words.
Explain why your device works.	Based on what you have learned in class, your data, and your life, why does your device do what I asked you to do?
Solve the problem. Explain your answer.	A rectangle has a perimeter of 36 units. One student says the rectangle with the greatest area is a square. How do you know this is correct?
Why is a roller coaster fun?	What makes a roller coaster fun? Justify how specific elements of the roller coaster add to the enjoyment of the ride.
Thinking about the character of the librarian, do you think she would have been an abolitionist? Why or why not?	Linking specific evidence and examples from the story and what you know about history, justify/explain why the librarian would have been or not been an abolitionist.

(Continued)

Explanation vs. Justification	
Explanation	*Justification*
How can we improve recycling in our school?	Justify how to improve the recycling within our school, providing specific steps and recommendations, with a rationale based on what you know about recycling and our school.
How did you find your answer?	Justify each step that you used to solve the problem, using what you know about math.
Why do you think a rabbit has a faster heartbeat than you?	Justify why a rabbit has a faster heartbeat than you based on our work in class, your research, and your experiment.
Why did your experiment work?	Explain why your experiment did or did not work. Your explanation should be based on facts you learned in our class and from additional research and should specifically be linked to aspects of your experiment.
Why did you like the piece of music?	Choose the most harmonious piece of music. Justify your choice based on our learning from class and your own experiences with music.
How does technology inform the workplace?	Justify how technology makes the workplace better, using specific information from our class, your own research, and information from the workplace interviews.

Notice that the word itself (explain or justify) is not as important as what the students are asked to do. In the justification column, students are moving beyond their opinion by providing specific information for their thoughts. You can use a simple question such as why, but you want to push students to move beyond the answer to a higher level.

A Final Note

Providing tasks and assignments that are at an appropriate level is a critical part of the productive struggle process. Theories such as Vygotsky's Zone of Proximal Development and Flow from Mihaly Csikszentmihalyi are helpful, as is choosing a suitable level of text. The characteristics of the task matter, as does requiring students to justify responses rather than simply explaining an answer.

Points to Ponder

1. How will you use the concepts of flow or the zone of proximal development?
2. How does the information related to levelled text impact your classroom?
3. What specific task characteristics are most applicable to your instruction?
4. How can you reword one of your questions to include justification?

Continue the Learning

Use the QR Code to access videos for your own use or for group professional development.

5

Scaffolding for Productive Struggle

General Scaffolding for Productive Struggle

Scaffolding is an integral part of productive struggle. There is a balance—supporting students without solving problems for them. This chapter has two main parts. First, we'll look at some general scaffolding strategies that are useful during productive struggle. Some may be used prior to the task; others may be used as needed during the task. You'll be the best person to determine that. Also, some scaffolding may be needed for certain students, rather than everyone. The goal is to scaffold when needed, but not if it takes away the productive part of the struggle. In the first part of the chapter, we'll discuss six general strategies.

> How to Scaffold the "Learning Together" Process
> Discourse During Productive Struggle
> Teaching Students to Activate Prior Knowledge
> Modeling Processes for Productive Struggle
> Supportive Questioning During Productive Struggle
> Providing Resources for Students

Then, in the second part, we'll revisit each of the productive struggle tasks from Chapter 4, this time with descriptions and examples of appropriate scaffolding.

How to Scaffold the "Learning Together" Process

Group work is one of the most effective ways to help students learn, especially in a productive learning setting. It can increase student motivation and is an important life skill. When I was teaching, some of my students didn't like to work in groups. They complained every day until I brought in a newspaper article that said the number one reason people were fired from their jobs was that they couldn't get along with their coworkers. That was an eye-opener for my students.

If you are going to ask students to work together in productive struggle, one of the ways to scaffold their success is to teach them how to work together. Let's consider five areas related to group work.

Areas Related to Group Work

Structures During Productive Struggle

Roles for Group Members

Rules for Working Together

Discourse During Productive Struggle

Questions to Prompt Discourse

Structures During Productive Struggle

First, determine how you want to organize your groups. Do you want students to work in pairs, groups of four, or some other organization? Will your students stay in the same group for a long period of time? I find that balance is important, and the task for productive struggle will often dictate what you should decide. For example, sometimes the task is most appropriate for partners, other times a larger group of four or five is effective.

I also think students should learn to work with the same people over time as well as learning to work with a variety of people, and they should not be limited to working with the same students all the time. In my classroom, I used groups of four for some activities and pairs for other activities. I switched my students around often enough that they rarely complained about other group members. They knew that I expected them to learn to work with everyone and that they would be grouped with someone else later.

Roles for Group Members

A critical step is structuring your group activity. Create an activity that requires each student to contribute to the task. It's important to assign roles for your students, although you may want students within a group to choose their roles. The roles may change depending on your assignment. For example, if students are working on a science experiment, you will need a safety monitor and a materials manager. However, if your project is developing visual model, you might prefer an artist.

Sample Roles and Responsibilities

Facilitator—Leader of the group; facilitates action
Recorder—Records comments and/or work
Reporter—Reports work to the entire group
Materials Manager—Collects and distributes materials
Timekeeper—Keeps the group working within time limits
Technology Manager—Coordinates technology use
Encourager—Encourages others
Summarizer—Summarizes work and may report to the class
Fact checker—Checks work from group; researches facts
Reflector—Reflects on comments from group, asks probing questions
Designer—Designs the project
Creator—Creates or builds the design

Here are some other possible subject-specific groups.

Sample Roles Within Math and Science Groups

- **Project Manager**—oversees the creation of subtasks and the delegation of each required task, while ensuring that individual members are working toward the big picture.
- **Strategy Analyst**—continuously monitors and reflects on the approach to completing a task, including the effectiveness of the strategies used by the group.
- **Reflector**—analyzes the work the group is doing, continuously reflecting on the efficiency of the group and its progress in meeting the task goals.

- **Recording Secretary**—ensures there's a written record of strategies, procedures, and data.
- **Materials Manager**—collects materials that are needed and returns them to the proper location after use.
- **Researcher**—designs a plan for how to obtain information and delegates search terms/tools to each member.
- **Data Collector**—records and organizes the data points for the group.
- **Progress Monitor**—checks scoring guides, directions, rubrics to ensure group is progressing toward goals in an efficient manner.
- **Friendly Critic**—looks for the mistakes, misconceptions, or calculation errors the group might be making and respectfully challenges the group to resolve inconsistencies together.

Sample Roles Within English Language Arts Groups

Discussion Leader—develops X questions (with answers and page references) at different levels. Leads discussion.

Artist—draws a picture that relates to the text and explains its significance.

Diction Detective—evaluates the diction used by identifying figurative language, imagery, and/or thematic statements and discusses the impact of the author's choice of words.

Craftsman—makes connections between the conflicts and characters and analyzes how they work together to drive the plot forward.

Sample Roles Within Social Studies Groups

Historical Preservationist—connects the text to a primary source document or other image that will deepen your understanding of the content.

Terminology Teacher—notes the academic terminology used in the text. Determines how to put it into a graphic organizer and provides examples/nonexamples to broaden peers' understanding of the concepts.

Connector—makes connections between the text we have read today and what we have discussed in class. Makes connections to how this relates to our previous unit in history and how it impacts the world we live in today.

I encourage you to rotate the roles within the team for different assignments so that one or two students do not dominate the group activities. You should also take time to teach students about their roles and responsibilities. This will ensure that the group process doesn't interfere with their productive struggle.

Rules for Working Together

In addition to your standard classroom rules, you may need a couple of simple rules that are specific to productive struggle group activities. I found that I needed to discuss my expectations for the noise level of the classroom. For example, I wanted my students to talk to each other. But they needed to talk to their group members, not the entire class. You might come up with a catchy way to describe an appropriate noise level, such as "Bees Buzz." Bees buzz when they are being productive (making honey), but they don't shout. I was in another classroom in which the teacher talked about using your "12-inch voice." Her students knew that meant that people within a foot (within the group) should be able hear you, but not those outside the group (more than a foot away).

I also used a rule called "ask three before me." This one works when your students are in groups of four. It simply means that a student should ask his or her group members for help before asking the teacher. This encourages students to look to each other for support instead of always looking to the teacher first. It's up to you to decide what rules you need in your classroom. Be sure that your students understand your expectations, and monitor the groups continuously to ensure that all students have an opportunity to participate. Here are sample rules I used.

Sample Group Rules

Respect Each Other

Listen To the Other Person Before You Speak

Ask Probing Questions When You Don't Understand

If You Want to Disagree, Be Prepared to Explain Your Perspective

Stay Positive

Finally, you may want to use talking chips, a strategy in which you give each student three chips or tokens. Each time a student speaks, he or she must turn in his or her chip (in a bag in the center of the group). When each student is out of chips, they are not allowed to talk until all other students have turned in their chips. This ensures participation from all students.

Discourse During Productive Struggle

Elements of Successful Discourse

Successful discourse is critical to productive struggle. Too often, we accept what is simply noise—students talking, perhaps off-topic, often over each other. That's not discourse. Discourse is "classroom talk." It is on-topic, it uses academic vocabulary, and students listen just as much as they talk. Let's look at the 9 characteristics of effective discourse.

> Disagreements are handled respectfully
> Indicators of success are well defined
> Students participate equally and equitably
> Clear directions are given
> Open-ended opportunities are provided
> Use of wait time and scaffolding is appropriate
> Raise the level of talk with academic vocabulary
> Students ask questions in addition to answering them
> Everyone is successful

In the following table, you can find a simple self-assessment for students to use regarding discourse.

Upper Grades Academic Conversations Expectations			
	Beginning	*Moving Forward*	*Expert*
Remarks	I shared my thoughts	I provided limited evidence for points I shared.	In addition to sharing my thoughts and evidence, I add new insights.
Responses	I listened to others' ideas	In addition to listening, I responded with a response that was on target.	After listening to others' responses, I ask clarifying questions, add new information, and make connections to other points in the conversation.
Reflection	I thought about what I heard my classmates say	As I thought about what was being said, I worked to make connections to other parts of the discussion and other learning.	After actively listening to my peers, I connect to learning in class and my own life to internalize the points.

Questions to Prompt Discourse During Productive Struggle

It's helpful to provide starter questions to help students discuss their productive struggle tasks.

Starter Questions
To Prompt More Thinking:
♦ You are on the right track. Tell us more.
♦ You are onto something. Keep going.
♦ The teacher said there is no right answer, so what would be your best answer?
To Fortify or Justify a Response
♦ What is your opinion about . . . ?
♦ Why is what you said important?
♦ Why do you think that?
♦ Explain how you got that answer.
To See Others' Points of View
♦ How is what you are thinking different from me?
♦ Do you see another way to do this?
To Consider Consequences
♦ How can we apply this to real life?
♦ What did you learn in another lesson that we can connect this too?
♦ How else can we use this?

Source: adapted from http://ptgmedia.pearsoncmg.com/images/9780205627585/downloads/Echevarria_math_Ch1_TheAcademicLanguageofMathematics.pdf

Here's another set for specific subject areas.

Sample Question Starters			
Language Arts	*Math*	*Science*	*Social Studies*
Which character . . . ?	When I compare . . . ?	Which reaction . . . ?	What led to . . . ?
Why did . . . ?	When I order . . . ?	If I did this again would . . . ?	Which events were . . . ?
If . . . ?	What information . . . ?	Why did this . . . ?	How did they . . . ?
Which clues . . . ?	Which phrases . . . ?	How did this . . . ?	Why did they . . . ?
Where did . . . ?	How do I . . . ?	How might the results change if . . . ?	How might things have been different if . . . ?
Which word or phrase . . . ?	I wonder if another solution . . . ?		
What event . . . ?			

Teaching Students to Activate Prior Knowledge

Helping students activate their prior knowledge can help them be more successful during productive struggle. You can use an anticipation guide or K-W-L.

Sample Anticipatory Guide–Theatre Arts		
Directions: Check whether the statement is true or false.		
Before Lesson	Statement	After Lesson
True ☐ False ☐	1. In theatre, the term "blocking" refers to the planned movement of actors on stage.	True ☐ False ☐
True ☐ False ☐	2. The "fourth wall" is an imaginary barrier between the actors and the audience.	True ☐ False ☐
True ☐ False ☐	3. A monologue is a dialogue between two characters.	True ☐ False ☐
True ☐ False ☐	4. Stage left and stage right are always the same from both the actor's and the audience's perspective.	True ☐ False ☐
True ☐ False ☐	5. A director is responsible for interpreting the script, guiding actors, and shaping the overall performance.	True ☐ False ☐

K-W-L Charts

Probably the most common method of activating students' prior knowledge that I see in classrooms today is a K-W-L chart. During a K-W-L activity, you ask the students what they already know about a topic (K) or what they think they know about it. Next, you ask what they want to know (W).

Then, you teach the lesson and ask them what they learned (L). You can also add an H—"How Can We Learn This" to create a K-W-H-L organizer.

K-W-H-L Chart			
K (what I know or think I know)	W (what I want to learn)	H (how I can learn this)	L (what I learned)

I particularly like the KWHL for productive struggle. Students can use the graphic to reflect on their knowledge and also plan a strategy for learning.

Modeling Processes for Productive Struggle

How often are your students confused? Mine were confused more often that I'd like to remember. Some of your students, particularly your struggling learners, need to understand what is happening in your head. They need you to show them what you think and how you think. Although important throughout your instruction, it's particularly important with productive struggle.

Modeling Thinking

If your students are working with online resources, we may need to model how to effectively "read" a website.

> When I look up information on the internet, I take time to read about the source to see if it is credible. Understanding biases is important. I go to the "About Me" and I see if they recommend any sources and I look for any references they use at the end of their content. I also want to be careful I don't get distracted from what I need to do, so I don't click on a lot of links or go to social media unless I have a specific purpose.

You can follow the same process with any instruction.

High School Math Think Aloud

Problem

A ball is thrown upward from a height of 5 feet with an initial velocity of 40 feet per second. The height h (in feet) after t seconds is given by:

$h(t) = -16t^2 + 40t + 5$

Question: How long will it take the ball to hit the ground?

Step 1: Restating the Problem

Okay, the function models height over time. I need to know when the ball hits the ground, which means the height is zero. I need to find the value of t when $h(t) = 0$.

Step 2: Setting Up the Equation

So I'll set the quadratic equal to zero: $-16t^2 + 40t + 5 = 0$.

Step 3: Deciding on a Method

I have three choices: solving by quadratic by factoring, completing the square, or the quadratic formula. Looking at it, factoring seems messy, so the quadratic formula is the best choice.

Step 4: Applying the Quadratic Formula

The quadratic formula is $(-b \pm \sqrt{(b^2 - 4ac)})/2a$. Here, a = −16, b = 40, c = 5.

Step 5: Calculating Discriminant

Now I need to solve the discriminant: $b^2 - 4ac = 40^2 - 4(-16)(5)$. That's 1600 + 320 = 1920. Since it's positive, there are two real solutions.

Step 6: Computing Roots

Now, $\sqrt{1920} \approx 43.82$. Plug into formula: $t = (-40 \pm 43.82)/-32$.

For the "plus" case: $(-40 + 43.82)/-32 = 3.82/-32 \approx -0.12$. That doesn't work because time can't be negative.

For the "minus" case: $(-40 - 43.82)/-32 = -83.82/-32 \approx 2.62$. That's positive, so it must be right.

> *Step 7: Reflection*
> That means the ball will hit the ground after about 2.6 seconds. I had to think about which root made sense. This is important: I can determine more than one answer, but only one fits the context.

See how simple it is? In fact, it's so automatic for us, we assume everyone else would know how to think through that process. Your strong students will be able to do that in their heads, but your struggling students will not understand. That's why it's important to model your thinking as needed during the productive struggle process.

Modeling With Video

Middle school teacher Jessica Neuberger uses modeling to prepare students for their first student-led portfolio assessment conferences. As she explains:

> I recorded a sample interview to give the students a good idea of what to expect. When the class viewed the sample interview, I would stop the video after each question, have the students repeat each question to me and then they would write it down. The second time through, we watched the whole interview with no interruptions. Then we discussed it. When I interviewed the students throughout the next week, they were prepared to share their work with me, offer me their opinions of their strengths and weaknesses, and we were able to set a goal for the next part of the year.

Because she knew this would be challenging for her students, she modeled the entire process for them and then provided scaffolded instruction to ensure their success. What I like about this is that the video could be available as students need it during the productive struggle process.

Supportive Questioning During Productive Struggle

One way to scaffold questions is by using other questions that lead to the answer. For example, simply asking "Where will a seed grow best?" can be supported with questions such as: "What do plants need to grow?" "Does light matter?" "How can you find out?"

The following is an example of how supporting questions can be used to guide students in reading the Declaration of Independence (https://www.archives.gov/founding-docs/declaration-transcript).

- What was the political situation of the American colonies in 1776?
- What are some rights you believe governments should guarantee to people?
- What do you think "independence" meant to the colonists at that time?
- What questions come up when you hear "Declaration of Independence"? What do you expect to find in the text?
- Who are the main audiences the Declaration is addressing (e.g. King George III, other colonies, citizens)?
- What grievances (complaints) are listed, and what kind of evidence is used to support them?
- How is the text structured (preamble, list of grievances, conclusion)? How does each section contribute?
- What phrases stand out as especially powerful or significant ("all men are created equal," etc.)? Why do they matter?
- Are there any terms or ideas that seem unfamiliar or ambiguous (e.g. "merciless Indian Savages," "jurisdiction," etc.)?

It's important to note that these questions don't provide the answer; they ask students to look for more narrow information that leads to the broader question. That's critical during productive struggle—you want to provide support without providing the answer to your students.

Providing Resources for Students

Providing ready-to-use resources is also important. Consider what students might need during the productive struggle process. Let's look at five types of resources.

> Friendly Dictionaries
> Word Walls
> Guide-o-Ramas
> Leveled Texts
> Graphic Organizers

First, I particularly like having friendly dictionaries available for students. There are a wide range available now, both in print and online such as Merriam-Webster's Word Central. I also like the Collins COBUILD Dictionary, which uses more student-friendly definitions for struggling learners.

If you teach something other than reading/language arts/English, much of your vocabulary is specialized, which likely has a unique meaning. Therefore, you need something different.

Vocabulary Resources	
Math	*Science*
Amathsdictionaryforkids.com Mathisfun.com (K-12) Mathwords.com Wolfram Math World	World of Science Enchanted Learning (includes specialized dictionaries such as astronomy and botany) Visionlearning Glossary NASA's Picture Dictionary
Social Studies	*Others*
Ancient History Encyclopedia Online Dictionary of the Social Sciences Geography Dictionary and Glossary (ISTE)	Netlingo (technology definitions) Sportsdefinitions.com** Museum of Modern Art dictionary Basic Art Dictionary (https://theartyteacher.com/art-dictionary/?srsltid=AfmBOoqOPLMw2Jr8qIm fr1s9alTJswTnwA9SRDKMxBDdK en7_tNn2gO9) Library Science (https://odlis.abc-clio.com) Naxos.com**(music) Music and Musicians/Orchestra. (https://en.wikisource.org/wiki/A_Dictionary_of_Music_and_Musicians/Orchestra On Music (https://dictionary.onmusic.org) Inc. Com Encyclopedia (business) Word Reference Languages (https://www.wordreference.com) Langenscheidt (https://en.langenscheidt.com)

(Continued)

Vocabulary Resources
Online Visual Dictionaries for Struggling Learners Vidtionary Kids Wordsmyth Wild (Spanish version available)

Word Walls

Another resource is word walls, which have been in favor for years. For example, when I was teaching I posted new spelling words on the ceiling. Finally, a student noticed, and they were intrigued that I not only posted the words, but left them up in case they needed help. My purpose, in part, was to teach them to find information when they needed it instead of just memorizing words. Ironically, they studied harder knowing they had extra assistance available.

I recommend having a specific word wall for your current instruction, including the task for productive struggle. Whether you are teaching vowel sounds, fractions, particles, types of government, or elements of art, there are key words and concepts your students need to know. You can post all the words in advance and refer to them throughout your lessons or post them as you teach. Be sure to place your words in a prominent place in your classroom.

Other Tips for Word Walls
Be sure your lettering is large enough to be seen throughout the room. Be careful with colors—yellow looks bright, but it doesn't work well for the words themselves. Put your word wall where students can see it clearly. Add pictures for English learners. Remove words once they are generally understood. Make room for new words.

You can also use personal word walls for students or groups. Using file folders, notebooks, or shared documents, students develop their own word walls based on the task, your instruction and guidance. I like using post-it notes for the words so students can rearrange them and remove words as needed.

Sample Personal or Group Word Wall	
General Words for the Topic	*Words for this Task*
Words I'm Working On	*Other Words*

Other Resources

Other Resources	
General	*Social Studies*
8 Tips for Creating Word Walls in Secondary: https://www.readingandwritinghaven.com/8-tips-for-creating-effective-word-walls-in-secondary How and Why to Use Word Walls with Older Students: https://buildingbooklove.com/how-and-why-to-use-word-walls-with/ Word Walls: Supporting Literacy in Secondary School Classrooms: https://www.readingrockets.org/sites/default/files/migrated/content/pdfs/World_Walls_-_A_Support_for_Literacy_in_Secondary_School_Classrooms.pdf Tips for Setting up Middle or High School Word Walls: https://www.brainyapples.com/2020/02/10/setting-up-a-word-wall-in-middle-high-school/	Word Walls in Social Studies: https://www.socialstudies.org/sites/default/files/view-article-2020-10/se-8405020313.pdf Using Word Walls Successfully in Social Studies: https://www.socialstudiessuccess.com/2016/12/using-word-walls-successfully-in-social-studies.html Early American History Word Wall: https://mrandmrssocialstudies.com/early-american-history-word-wall-a-how-to-guide/

Other Resources	
Math	*Science*
Mathematics Vocabulary Word Wall Cards (free) all grades: https://www.doe.virginia.gov/teaching-learning-assessment/k-12-standards-instruction/mathematics/instructional-resources/mathematics-vocabulary-word-wall-cards High School Math Word Wall Ideas: https://www.scaffoldedmath.com/2015/09/high-school-math-word-wall-ideas.html Middle School Math Word Wall Ideas: https://www.scaffoldedmath.com/2017/10/middle-school-math-word-wall-ideas.html	Science Word Walls: https://theteachersupstairs.com/science-word-walls-2-painless-ways-to-effectively-use-them/ The Evolution of my Middle School Science Word Wall: https://keslerscience.com/the-evolution-of-my-middle-school-science-word-wall Using Word Walls in Science: https://www.socialstudiessuccess.com/2016/12/using-word-walls-successfully-in-social-studies.html
Other	
Word Walls in the Music Classroom: https://study.com/academy/popular/music-word-walls.html My Music Classroom Has a Word Wall, Now What? http://melodysoup.blogspot.com/2012/09/my-music-classroom-has-word-wall-now.html?showComment=1347924792531 Taxonomy of Music Graphic: https://turnerkarl.wordpress.com/2012/10/11/finished-music-infographic/ Physical Education Word Walls: https://www.capnpetespowerpe.com/single-post/how-to-use-word-walls-in-physical-education-tips-and-strategies PE Word Wall: https://www.thephysedteacher.com/pe-word-wall.html	

Guide-o-Rama

Whether you are asking students to read a portion of text, you will also want to model your thinking. It's important to provide a guide. Otherwise, students won't know what to look for. These can be detailed, or more general. If you blend a think-aloud with study guide notes, it is very effective for students to use in group, partner, or individual work. Guide-o-Ramas combine a study guide with a think-aloud.

Guide-O-Rama *Europe: War and Change, Chpt. 12 (Sections 12.1 and 12.2)*	
Page	*Reading Tip*
326	Look at the map provided. I bet the location of Great Britain impacted its involvement in World War II. This might be something I want to watch for in the text as I read.
328	There are so many causes and effects of World War II, but they are scattered throughout the next several pages. I think it would be helpful to keep track of them all in one place. Let's make a two-column box to bullet point them as we notice them in the text.
329–332	As I read this section, I immediately see bolded terms that look unfamiliar: nationalism, colonialism and dual monarchy. I need to see how these terms relate to WWII and how they differ. I'm certainly going to address these in my notes!
334–338	There seem to be a lot of dates on these pages. As I read this section, I'm going to make a timeline of which countries joined the war and possibly what motivated them to join.
335	I found it interesting that dogs were used in the war to detect mines and guard ammunition! I'm not sure I think this was humane. What other alternatives would have been better options?

	Guide-O-Rama *Europe: War and Change, Chpt. 12 (Sections 12.1 and 12.2)*
Page	*Reading Tip*
336	The term "fascism" is a term I've never heard before. I wonder how this compares to what I already know about communism and democracy. I'm going to look for this as I read.
338	There seem to be multiple factors that contributed to the rapid growth of the Soviet Union. Some seem more significant than others. I think I'll rank them in order of significance.

They are also useful with videos.

Guide-O-Rama

Ratios (https://youtu.be/UxWsY59NVgc)

Time #	*Reading Tip*
0 seconds	What do you already know about ratios? Before I watch a video, I also write down what I'm confused about or what I want to learn.
15 seconds	How does the tutor define ratios? How does it compare to your thoughts? For me, sometimes it doesn't match, so I know I need to pay extra attention to the video.
51 seconds	The first time I watched this, I was a little confused because writing a ratio looks exactly like writing a fraction. Did this confuse you?
1:40	Stop and think for a minute. Is this making sense? If it is confusing, you might want to back up the video now and re-watch it. I've found that it helps me to stop when I don't understand a step rather than waiting until the end.

Following, you'll find tips for building a guide-o-rama, which should only be used when students have moved beyond productive struggle to frustration. Use them judiciously. Also, for young students, I've found it more effective to give them the steps one at a time, rather than all at once.

How to Build a Guide-O-Rama

1. Identify a chunk of content you need students to read. Guide-o-ramas should be used with challenging texts that you anticipate students will struggle with.
2. Determine guiding questions that will help them process key portions of the text, similar to what you would use in a traditional study guide.
3. Add think-aloud comments, such as "Notice that on page 56, there is a box of math or science symbols. When I see a box of text in the margin, I pay special attention since it usually contains important information." These are typically questions and/or statements that you would verbally use to model your thinking for students.
4. Use visuals that will help students remember the content. For example, if students are reading about the Pythagorean Theorem, you might put each question in a right triangle.
5. Keep in mind that your goal is twofold: help students process and understand the complex text and move toward independence in learning.

Providing Layered Text

A particular concern in the middle and high school classroom occurs when students cannot read grade-level text. Sometimes you must start with easier text in order to build to more complex text, which will deepen understanding. One strategy for supporting students during productive struggle who are not reading at grade level is "layering meaning." This strategy can be used for any student who cannot yet read the grade-level or assigned text material because it allows students to read another text on the same topic that is written at an easier level. Students read that selection first to build their own prior knowledge and vocabulary; then they can go back and read the more complex text with your support. It's an excellent strategy, one that encourages high levels of challenge because students move beyond the easier text, but one that requires texts at differing levels. A variety of websites provide leveled texts for your use.

Sources for Leveled Text

**Right now, unless noted, these are free, but they may add premium items or add a fee at a later time.

Reading A to Z (https://www.readinga-z.com/books/leveled-books/) provides a variety of books and passages. KidsNews (https://www.kidsnews.com.au) is a terrific site in Australia that is designed for kids and their parents.

CommonLit (www.commonlit.org), News in Levels (http://www.newsinlevels.com), and FortheTeachers (http://www.fortheteachers.org/reading_skills/) also provide varying levels of an article or text. For the teachers has science, health, and other topics, but information is language arts oriented. Reading Vine (https://www.readingvine.com/passages/skill/) provides text by levels.

DodNews (dogonews.com) is particularly appropriate for middle school students.

TweenTribune (http://tweentribune.com) is produced by the Smithsonian. It is now archived, but may be helpful.

Readworks (http://www.readworks.org) is a little different—they do texts, including paired texts, but they do **not** provide differing levels of the same text.

Text Compactor (http://www.textcompactor.com) lets you paste text into it and then automatically summarizes it (with a customized setting you control).

Rewordify (http://rewordify.com) allows a teacher or student to paste text into the screen, and it will identify challenging words and replace them with explanations.

Diffit is an AI tool (free for most features; premium available) which allows you to enter text and ask for differing levels.

Paraphrase (https://paraphrasetool.com/modes/shorten-paraphrasing-tool?gclid=CjwKCAiA04arBhAkEiwAuNOsIsINpv_vaLwLiaY3beAl06Qji80Eyt8NrvaQmUeb4cg1C2iZAy5CZBoC2s4QAvD_BwE) does exactly that—generally shortening the text.

Graphic Organizers

Graphic organizers are an excellent resource for students. They help students organize their information visually and chunk information that might be overwhelming. Having graphic organizers available tied to the productive struggle task is an excellent resource. Later in the chapter, you'll see specific examples tied to the tasks from Chapter 4. Here's let's look at several general samples.

I particularly like a graphic organizer to understand vocabulary.

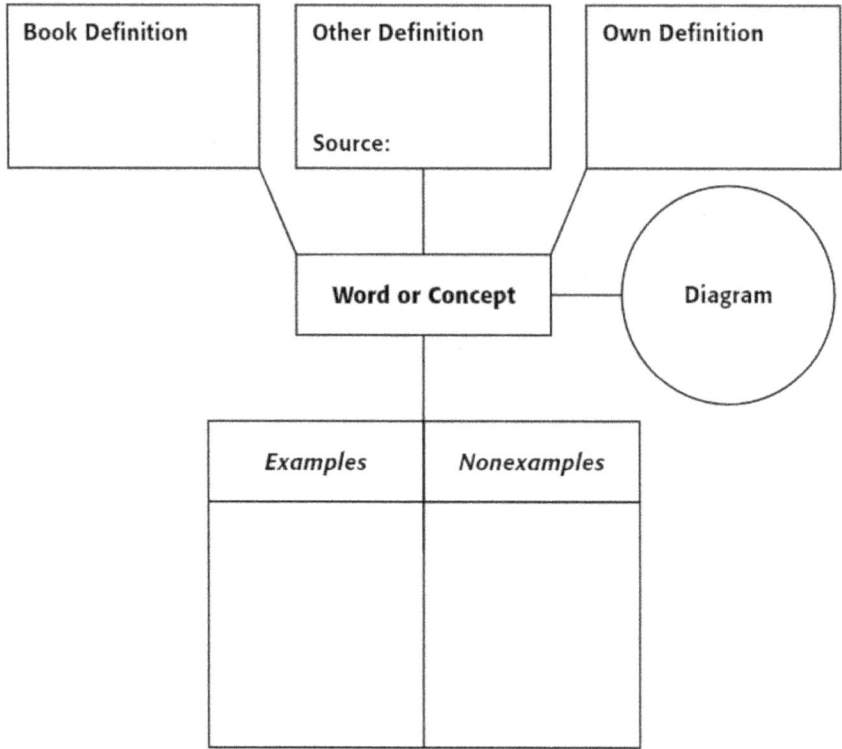

Next, let's look a comparison sample for English.

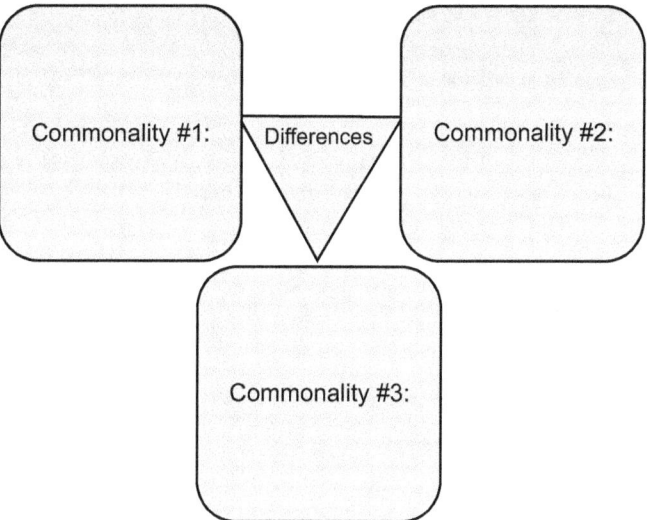

Comparison between Romeo and Juliet vs. West Side Story

A mathematics teacher used design elements to teach the Pythagorean Theorem.

Sample Pythagorean Theorem

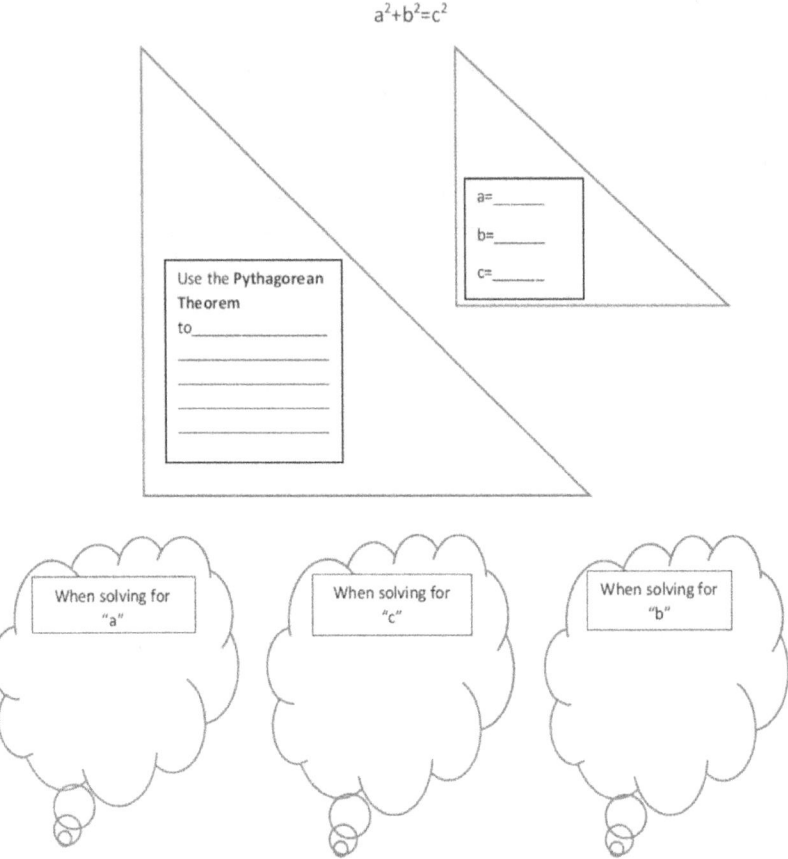

Dividing a sheet of paper into all the aspects related to a specific event can be helpful in a Social Studies classroom.

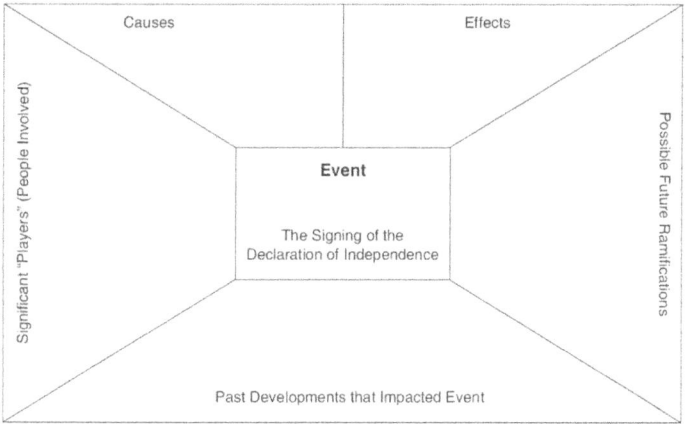

Next, let's look at a word wheel for a Spanish classroom.

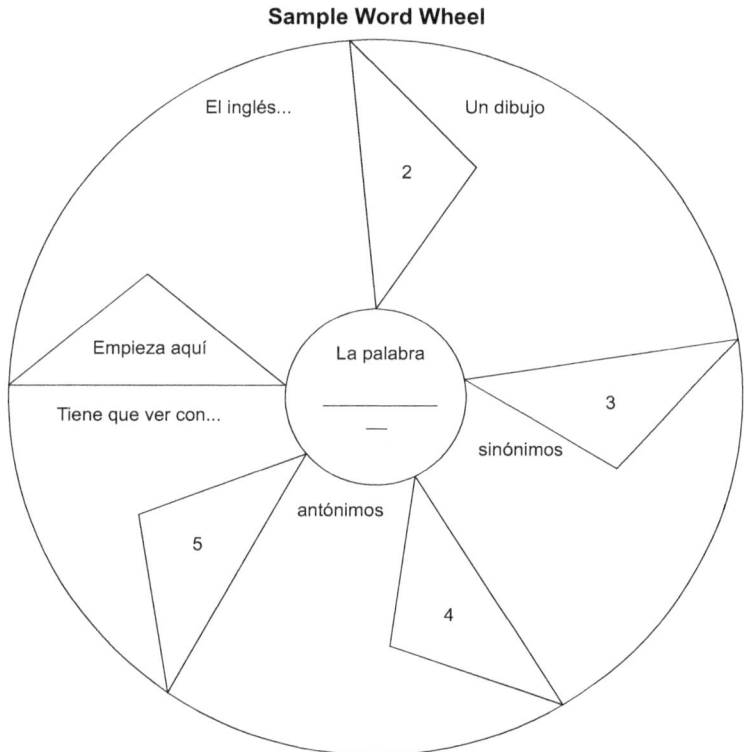

La rueda de una palabra...The word wheel
Empieza aquí...Start here
El inglés... The English
Un dibujo...A drawing
Sinónimos...synonyms
Antónimos...antonyms
Tiene que ver con...It has to do with (other related words)

Scaffolding for Productive Struggle ◆ 135

Finally, check out a music design from a class of middle schoolers.

Teaching Students to Self-Scaffold

One of the best ways to scaffold learning through productive struggle is to teach students to self-scaffold. Ideally, anytime you use a scaffolding strategy you use it in a way that teaches students how to independently use it. However, there are three specific ways to teach students to self-scaffold.

Question Starters

First, keep a bank of question starters in a readily available place for students. Earlier in the chapter I provided samples you can use. Here is another excellent tool, the question matrix, which provides students a wide range of question starters. You can run these on cardstock, cut them apart and put in envelopes or bags, and students can draw questions to prompt a discussion.

Question Matrix						
What Is	When Is	Where Is	Which Is	Who Is	Why Is	How Is
What Did	When Did	Where Did	Which Did	Who Did	Why Did	How Did

(Continued)

Question Matrix						
What Is	When Is	Where Is	Which Is	Who Is	Why Is	How Is
What Can	When Can	Where Can	Which Can	Who Can	Why Can	How Can
What Would	When Would	Where Would	Which Would	Who Would	Why Would	How Would
What Will	When Will	Where Will	Which Will	Who Will	Why Will	How Will
What Might	When Might	Where Might	Which Might	Who Might	Why Might	How Might

Source: Wiederhold (1995)

Graphic Organizers

Next, graphic organizers are a key resource for students. Although there are times you will want to provide an organizer designed for the specific task, there are also general organizers you may keep available for students at all times. Giving them tips for choosing a graphic organizer is helpful.

Choosing a Graphic Organizer	
Question	*Type of Graphic Organizer*
Do you need to summarize 2 topics?	T-Chart
Do you need to compare and contrast?	Venn Diagram
Do you need to summarize information for different topics?	Semantic Feature Analysis
Do you want to describe a sequence?	Sequence Chart

Determining When I Need Help

Finally, you want to teach students to scaffold for themselves before asking you for help. I used the following reminders to help them make that decision.

	How to Get Help
Try It On Your Own	What exactly do I need help with? Have I learned something similar before? What have I learned that will help me? Is there anything on our walls that will help? Is there anything in our classroom resource kit that can help?
Work with Others	Can anyone in my group help me? Can we work together to solve the problem? Do we need to ask someone not in our group? Who might know the answer?
Ask the Teacher	I've tried on my own, and I've asked other people. Can you help me now?

Applying Scaffolding to Productive Struggle Activities

Now, let's look at how scaffolding applies to particular productive struggle activities. We're going to return to each of the tasks from Chapter 4, adding specific scaffolding strategies. At times, I'll simply note a strategy, such as modeling. Other times, such as using graphic organizers, I'll provide a sample for your use.

Middle School Math

Three-Statement Method
1. The best solution is attempt number . . .
2. This is because . . .
3. The reason(s) the other attempts are not as strong . . .

For this middle school math example, modeling the decision process is critical. You could also use a standard graphic organizer to help them process their choices.

Middle School Math Graphic Organizer		
Problem	*This Makes Sense Because . . .*	*This Doesn't Make Sense Because . . .*
1.		
2.		
3.		

> **High School Math**
>
> *Pythagorean Theorem . . . What Is That?*
>
> Thanks to Pythagoras, we have a great equation that we can use to find the length of the sides of a right triangle. The theorem is used in architecture, navigation and surveying, which are important parts of our lives, but what if Pythagoras had never come up with the theorem? Sure, you could use measurement of a tool, but some things may be impossible to measure such as if you are trying to find distances between long navigation points. For instance, a plane can use its height above the ground and its distance from the destination airport to find the correct place to begin a descent to that airport. It seems like something is left out. Your charge is to come up with a replacement equation that would assist you with the following problem. You should be able to explain how you came up with the new equation and also include the drawbacks of using this equation. Pythagoras can't be replaced, but I bet you can come close.
>
> Your grandmother is moving in with you and needs wheel access to your home. The height of your current porch steps are 4.5ft. Your dad said that he thinks the ramp needs to be 10ft long. Based on your dad's guess, would you be able to build the ramp to meet these specifications? Explain how you came up with a new equation instead of Pythagorean Theorem to solve this equation. Include the drawbacks of using this equation.
>
> https://sciencing.com/real-life-uses-pythagorean-theorem-8247514.html

The assignment asking student to create an alternative to the Pythagorean Theorem is complex, and may need several scaffolding tools. A simple T-chart can help students think about what they need to do.

Pythagorean Theorem T-Chart	
Characteristics of the Pythagorean Theorem	*Characteristics I Need to Include in My Plan*

A detailed graphic organizer can also help them organize their information.

High School Math Graphic Organizer	
My Dad's Guess: Your dad said that he thinks the ramp needs to be 10ft long.	
My Proposed Plan:	
How I Came Up with My Plan:	
Benefits to My Plan	Drawbacks to My Plan

> ### *Middle School Science*
>
> Design an investigation to test the effects of temperature on how enzymes break down food with limited materials.

In addition to modeling how to design an investigation, a checklist is helpful.

> ### *Middle School Scientific Investigation Checklist*
>
> **Step 1: Question and Hypothesis**
> - ☐ Did I write a clear question that can be tested?
> - ☐ Did I make a prediction (hypothesis) in an if . . . then . . . because format?
>
> **Step 2: Variables**
> - ☐ Did I identify what I will change (independent variable)?
> - ☐ Did I identify what I will measure (dependent variable)?
> - ☐ Did I list what I will keep the same (controls)?
>
> **Step 3: Materials and Safety**
> - ☐ Do I have all the materials I need?
> - ☐ Did I think about safety rules and write them down?
>
> **Step 4: Procedure**
> - ☐ Did I write clear, step-by-step directions?
> - ☐ Will someone else be able to follow my steps?
> - ☐ Did I plan to repeat the test at least three times?
>
> **Step 5: Data**
> - ☐ Do I have a table or chart ready to collect data?
> - ☐ Did I include the units (seconds, centimeters, etc.)?
> - ☐ Did I plan to write down observations as well as numbers?
>
> **Step 6: Results and Conclusion**
> - ☐ Do I know how I will show my results (graph, chart, table)?
> - ☐ Did I write how I will decide if my hypothesis was supported?
> - ☐ Did I plan to explain what I learned and what I might do differently?

You may also want to have a data collection sheet available.

Data Collection Sheet: Temperature and Enzyme Activity

Investigation Question

How does temperature affect the rate at which enzymes break down food?

Hypothesis

If _____, then _____ because _____.

Materials Used (List What You Actually Have Available)

- _____
- _____
- _____

Variables

Independent Variable (what I change): _____

Dependent Variable (what I measure): _____

Controlled Variables (things I keep the same):

1. _____
2. _____
3. _____

Data Table

Trial #	Temperature (°C/°F)	Food sample used	Time for food to break down (sec/min)	Observations (color, texture, bubbles, etc.)
1				
2				
3				
4				

(Add rows as needed)

Average Results

Temperature (°C/°F)	Average Breakdown Time	Notes

Reflection

1. What trend do you see in your data?
   _____

2. Did your results support your hypothesis? Why or why not?
   _____

3. What would you change if you did this experiment again?
   _____

High School Science

You are a scientist researching new vaccines to combat viruses in our society. Research the benefits and disadvantages on all stakeholders, including analyzing biases that exist. Then, create a proposed set of vaccine development guidelines to send to the CDC that are justified by scientific evidence rather than opinion.

First, students may need a checklist for reference.

Checklist for Researching a Topic

Identify your topic

Note any related areas that will inform your research

Identify key sources

Determine any biases that exist with sources

Ensure you have enough variety in research sources that you can balance any biases

Look for sources that are referenced by other sources

Look for sources from credible organizations

Be aware of propaganda: it's not a solid source

They may also benefit from a notes frame.

Notes Frame	
Source:	
How I Know This Source is Credible:	
Summary of Key Information:	
Questions I Have:	
Benefits Described by This Perspective:	Disadvantages/Dangers Described From This Perspective:
Additional Information:	

Finally, a T-Chart can help students finalize their vaccine development guidelines.

T-Chart	
Recommendation/Guideline	*Evidence*

Middle School Social Studies

Analyze two historical primary sources that provide information about the same historical event. Explore biases and determine which of the two is a more reliable source, justifying their choice with evidence.

Again, a checklist is helpful.

Quick Bias Checklist

Use this short checklist to quickly decide if a source may be biased.

- ☐ Do I know who created this?
- ☐ What is their purpose (inform, persuade, entertain, sell)?
- ☐ Does it use emotional or loaded words?
- ☐ Is it fact or opinion?
- ☐ Are claims supported by facts or data?
- ☐ Are other viewpoints missing?
- ☐ Can I confirm this with another reliable source?
- ☐ Am I believing this just because it matches what I already think?

A graphic organizer can also help students coordinate their thoughts.

Graphic Organizer for Student Thoughts	
Source:	
Why This Source Is More Reliable	Why This Source Is Less Reliable
Source:	
Why This Source Is More Reliable	Why This Source Is Less Reliable
Which Source Is More Reliable (include evidence):	

High School Social Studies

Students divide into small groups, each selecting and researching a global, national, state, or even local issue. Students should also research the special-interest groups that have formed around this issue, noting their size, their constituency, and their messages and activities during the primaries or recent elections. Afterward, students form their own special-interest group. They must develop an agenda to promote their interest, arguments for their goals, and refutations against possible opposition points. Students must include a written rationale for their position that addresses the previous points. It must include specific, factual evidence from two or three credible sources. Finally, students create a 2- to 4-minute persuasive infomercial advocating for their point of view. It should include real-life examples of how the issue affects people's lives, as well as how supporting their issue is a solution to actual problems.

As students are researching special interest groups, a semantic feature analysis is helpful for comparison of groups.

Semantic Feature Analysis					
Group	Pro/Con on Issue	Size	Constituency	Message(s)	Activities
SI Group One					
SI Group Two					

When planning the infomercial, a graphic organizer may be helpful.

My Points

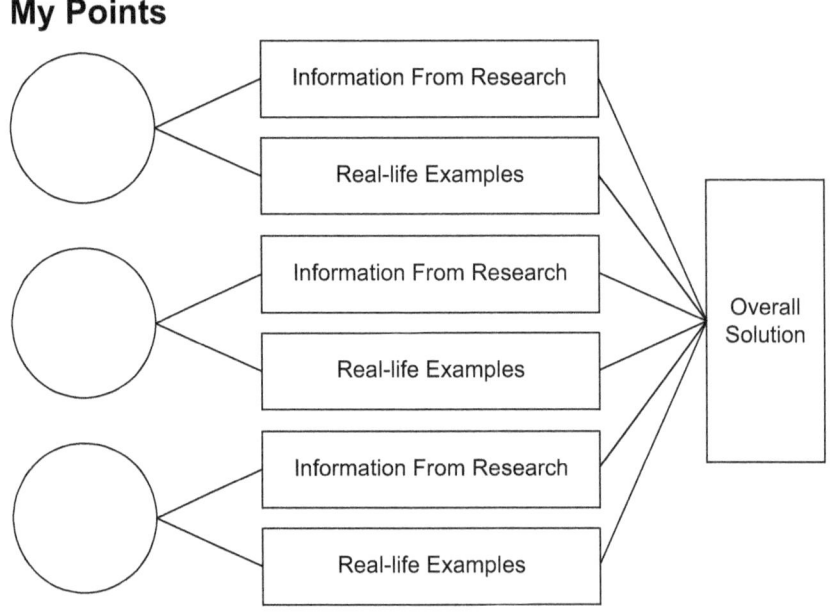

Finally, a tip sheet on persuasion may also be beneficial for planning.

Tips for Persuasion

Know Your Audience
- Think: Who am I trying to convince?
- Use examples, stories, or references that connect with them.
- Avoid talking down—respect your audience's opinions, even if they differ.

Start Strong
- Begin with a hook: a surprising fact, a question, or a short story.
- Clearly state your claim or opinion early on.

Use Logic
- Support your points with evidence such as facts, statistics, or real-life examples.
- Organize ideas step by step so the reasoning is easy to follow.
- Anticipate counterarguments and explain why your view still makes sense.

Appeal to Emotions
- Use vivid words and examples that make people feel something (fairness, pride, concern, hope).
- Tell a brief story that shows why your argument matters in real life.

Build Credibility
- Show that you know what you're talking about.
- Use trustworthy sources or explain personal experiences.
- Speak or write with confidence—but stay respectful.

Use Persuasive Techniques
- Repetition: Repeat key words or phrases to make them memorable.
- Rhetorical questions: Ask questions that make the audience think.
- Compare/contrast: Show how your option is better than another.
- Call to action: End by telling your audience what they should do or believe.

> **Middle School English/Language Arts**
>
> What is the theme of *Goldilocks and the Three Bears*? Use details from the text to support your choice. It was written nearly 200 years ago. Justify whether this theme applies to today. Provide an example from modern life to validate your answer.

It's important to model how to use details from the text to support a choice. Some students will also benefit from chunking information.

Chunking Information		
Theme	*Details from Text*	*Relevance to Today*

> **High School English/Language Arts**
>
> We have been reading dystopian novels. You have been given the opportunity to start a new society on a deserted island that is fully equipped with all needed amenities and modern technology. The island is not owned or under the influence of any nation. It is the responsibility of your group to inhabit the island in any manner that you choose. By completing the following assignments and working cooperatively, your group will build the perfect society and will introduce your society to the class.
>
> ♦ Note characteristics of healthy societies and governments (past and present) through online research.
> ♦ Note the pitfalls of unhealthy societies and governments (past and present) through online research.
> ♦ Determine the criteria you think would make the perfect society (type of government, freedoms, laws, technology available, etc.).
> ♦ Create a multimedia campaign advertising your community to the rest of the world. Use persuasive appeals but justify your choices with evidence from research you conducted and the books we have read in book clubs.

One tool that can help with comparisons is a semantic feature analysis.

Societies Semantic Feature Analysis		
	Healthy Societies and Governments	*Unhealthy Societies and Governments*
Past Characteristics		
Present Characteristics		

Then, a T-Chart can help as students develop the perfect society.

Societies T-Chart	
What I Want In A Society	*What I Don't Want In A Society*

A checklist reminder of persuasive techniques (also used in the high school social studies example earlier) is also beneficial.

Tips for Persuasion

Know Your Audience
- Think: Who am I trying to convince?
- Use examples, stories, or references that connect with them.
- Avoid talking down—respect your audience's opinions, even if they differ.

Scaffolding for Productive Struggle ◆ 151

Start Strong
- Begin with a hook: a surprising fact, a question, or a short story.
- Clearly state your claim or opinion early on.

Use Logic
- Support your points with evidence such as facts, statistics, or real-life examples.
- Organize ideas step by step so the reasoning is easy to follow.
- Anticipate counterarguments and explain why your view still makes sense.

Appeal to Emotions
- Use vivid words and examples that make people feel something (fairness, pride, concern, hope).
- Tell a brief story that shows why your argument matters in real life.

Build Credibility
- Show that you know what you're talking about.
- Use trustworthy sources or explain personal experiences.
- Speak or write with confidence—but stay respectful.

Use Persuasive Techniques
- Repetition: Repeat key words or phrases to make them memorable.
- Rhetorical questions: Ask questions that make the audience think.
- Compare/contrast: Show how your option is better than another.
- Call to action: End by telling your audience what they should do or believe.

Foreign Language

Translate a short story that includes idioms that do not have direct equivalents.

Modeling is critical when teaching students to translate from one language to another. Another helpful tool is a checklist for translation.

Tips for Translating When There Is No Direct Translation

Understand the Context
- Look at the sentence around the word—what is happening?
- Ask: Is the word describing an action, a feeling, or a cultural idea?
- Sometimes the meaning changes depending on context, not just the dictionary definition.

Explain the Meaning in More Words
- Instead of trying to find "one word," use a short phrase.
- Example: The German word Schadenfreude = "the feeling of happiness at someone else's misfortune."
- Using a phrase gives the sense even if it's not exact.

Use an Analogy or Example
- If the idea doesn't exist in English, explain it by comparison.
- Example: A food or tradition might be explained as "like ___, but with ___ difference."

Keep the Original Word (With Explanation)
- Sometimes the best option is to keep the foreign word and add a note or explanation.
- Example: Siesta (Spanish) can stay in Spanish, but you add "a short rest or nap taken in the afternoon."

Focus on the Feeling or Function
- If it's an emotion word, describe the feeling.
- If it's an object or action, describe what it does or how it's used.

Know That Some Words Carry Culture
- Some words are tied to culture, history, or traditions.
- Instead of "replacing" them, explain why they matter in that culture.
- Example: Hygge (Danish) is more than "coziness"—it's about warmth, comfort, and togetherness.

Don't Worry About Perfection
- The goal is to communicate the meaning, not to find a "perfect twin word."
- It's okay to say, "This doesn't translate directly, but it means . . ."

Technology

Your school newspaper wants to feature a series of articles about student life. You are part of a data mining team tasked with finding trends such as study habits, sleep, extracurricular activities, and social media use that might inform how schools should support students. Identify how you will collect data, how you will identify trends, and then do an investigation for the articles.

Because this productive struggle task requires multiple steps, students may need help breaking down the task. First, a T-Chart helps brainstorm trends and data sources.

Technology T-Chart	
Trend	*Data Sources*

Next, they can use a graphic organizer to collect data and form a preliminary conclusion.

Data source
Students draw lines from the appropriate data source to trends

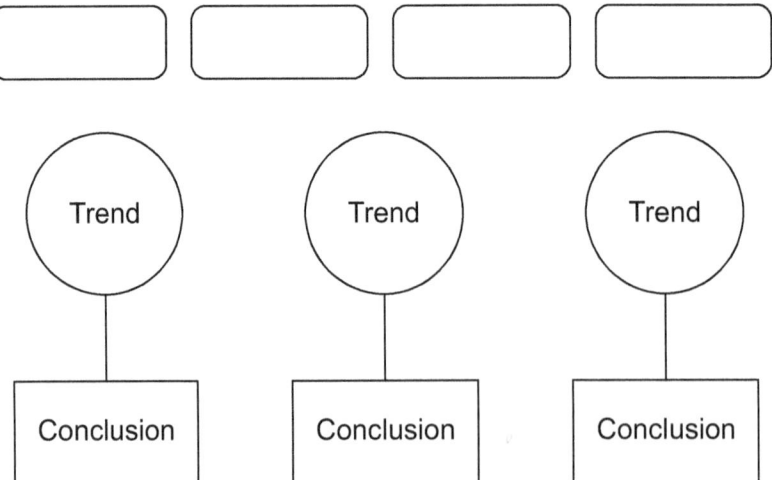

154 ◆ Productive Struggle in the 6–12 Classroom

Art

Students move through an art gallery of work created by their classmates. Each student chooses one piece of art and writes a short critique. The critique must include the student's opinion of the artwork, support of the opinion based on the lesson taught by the teacher and the student's own experiences, and recommendations for improvement.

Prior to students starting this task, it's important to show students models of good and bad critiques. As students are working together, they can use a T-Chart to brainstorm what should be included in their critiques.

Art T-Chart	
Include This ...	*Not This ...*

A graphic organizer may help students frame their evaluations and critiques.

Evaluations and Critiques Graphic Organizer	
My Opinion:	
Evidence from Our Class/Learning	Evidence from My Art Experience

(Continued)

Evaluations and Critiques Graphic Organizer	
My Recommendation:	
Evidence from Our Class/ Learning	Evidence from My Art Experience

> **Chorus**
>
> Groups are provided a piece with unexpected harmonies and other notes for them to master.

A creative way to help them think about how to deal with this is Start/Finish the Tip.

> **How Musicians Handle Unexpected Harmonies**
> _____First
> Adjust Your _____
> Lean on _____
> Use _____
> Rehearse _____
> Stay _____

Students brainstorm what the tips would be to help them deal with the unexpected harmonies.

> **Key**
>
> *How Musicians Handle Unexpected Harmonies*
> Listen First
> Adjust Your Pitch or Chord
> Lean on Your Learning from Class
> Use Improvisation
> Rehearse Problem Solving
> Stay Calm

> **Band**
>
> Provide a piece of music with missing measures, rests, or intentionally altered rhythms. Students must "fill in the gaps" by predicting or composing what belongs, testing their understanding of harmony, rhythm, and style.

In the band example, modeling this in advance is one of the best scaffolding tools. You might also use a sentence prompts to help students brainstorm what to do.

> **Sentence Prompts**
>
> *I Can Figure Out What To Do*
> I Can Try To . . .
> If That Doesn't Work . . .
> I Can Also . . .

> **Physical Education**
>
> Develop a series of tests to measure a student's fitness level. After you receive the results, interpret the results and develop a long-term fitness plan for the student.

Students might benefit from using a T-Chart to brainstorm possible tests to use to develop the plan.

Physical Education T-Chart	
Possible Test	*What It Measures*

They could also use a graphic organizer to pull together the information for the plan.

Physical Education Graphic Organizer	
Tests	*Results*
Fitness Activity	*Based on Which Results*
Overall Fitness Plan:	

> **Theatre Arts**
>
> In small groups, create a playbill to show that you understand all the components that go into a production. You'll also get a taste for marketing. Be sure you include costume descriptions, set descriptions, plot summary, fake cast and crew lists, and an evocative cover design. Also, write a paper justifying your choices and the impact you hope it would make on your audience.

Scaffolding might begin by helping students decide what to include and how it will appeal to the audience.

Theatre Arts Scaffolding	
Components to Include	*How to Appeal to the Audience*

You also may want to help break down the justification portion of the assignment.

Justification Breakdown		
Component	*Justification from Class/Learning*	*Justification from Life/Experience*

Career and Technical Education

You are the owner of a business that recycles computer equipment. Your driving purpose is: "How can we utilize older computer equipment in economical, business-connected ways?"

Create a business plan that addresses how to re-use older equipment in an economical, business-connected way. Include if there is some equipment that should just be disposed of, the impacts to the business community and environment of disposal, the costs of re-utilizing old equipment, and the benefits and disadvantages of re-using older equipment in an economical, business-connected way. Be specific as to how you would re-use the equipment so that it meets the criteria.

Career and Technical Education Graphic Organizer

Possible Way to Re-Utilize Computer	Economic Impact	Impact on Business

You might also provide a semantic feature analysis to compare the disposal aspect of the task.

Career and Technical Education Semantic Feature Analysis

Technology	Economic Impact	Business Impact	Advantages of Disposal	Disadvantages of Disposal

Family and Consumer Sciences

Develop a healthy eating plan for a family of three on a fixed budget (determined in advance). It's also important that one of the three family members is a diabetic. The healthy plan should include nutritious and tasty choices for all members.

Modeling how to make choices to meet a family's needs is a critical precursor to students' making decisions. Additionally, a template students can use to help design the eating plan can help students.

Eating Plan Template		
Consideration	*Include This*	*Do Not Include This*
Healthy Food		
Tasty		
Diabetic Person		
Cost		

Agricultural Education

Given a small plot of land, plan a crop rotation, balancing all related considerations including balancing soil health, yield, and potential setbacks. Justify your choices.

T-Charts are helpful with this productive struggle task.

Agricultural Education T-Chart	
What do I need to consider in my plan?	*What impact will that have?*

Specific aspects of my plan	*Justification for each aspect*

Media/Journalism

After researching two media sources that have different perspectives, analyze which of the two is more credible. Justify your decision with evidence from the sources, at least one more source, and your own experiences.

The bias checklist sheet I provided in the previous middle school social studies example is helpful here too.

Quick Bias Checklist

Use this short checklist to quickly decide if a source may be biased.

- ☐ Do I know who created this?
- ☐ What is their purpose (inform, persuade, entertain, sell)?
- ☐ Does it use emotional or loaded words?
- ☐ Is it fact or opinion?
- ☐ Are claims supported by facts or data?
- ☐ Are other viewpoints missing?
- ☐ Can I confirm this with another reliable source?
- ☐ Am I believing this just because it matches what I already think?
  A graphic organizer to chunk justification is also useful.

Media/Journalism Justification Chunking		
My Decision:		
Justification From Original Source(s)	Justification From Other Source	Justification From My Experience

Debate/Speech

Choose a side for a debate. Then, participate in a debate in which you argue the other side.

To scaffold a debate, a standard graphic organizer is helpful.

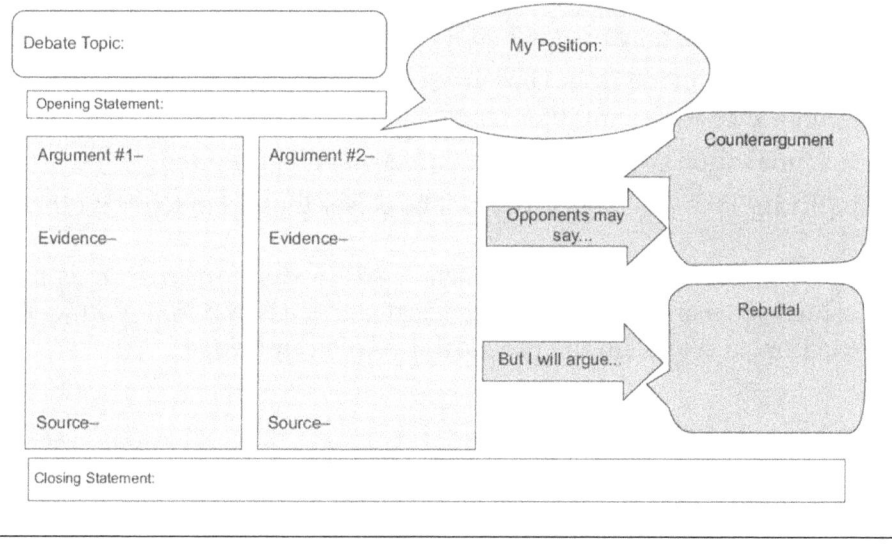

Engineering/Makerspace

Objective

Working in teams of two, design and build a bridge using balsa wood to hold as much weight as possible over a span of 30 cm while using the least amount of material.

Constraints

1. The overall width of the bridge must be at least 7 cm and may not exceed 10 cm.
2. The overall length of the bridge must be at least 33 cm long and may not exceed 35 cm.
3. The overall height of the bridge must be at least 7 cm and may not exceed 35 cm.
4. A block (8 cm long, 5 cm wide, 1.9 cm thick) must be able to pass through the bridge. Think of this as a car. This block will be used for applying a load to your bridge.
5. The bridge shall allow a 3/8-inch bolt to pass through the center of the bridge deck. This will be used for applying a load to your bridge.
6. Glue may only be used at the joints of the wood members.
7. Wood joints may be notched if desired.
8. If gussets made from card stock are used, they must be used on both sides of a joint in order to reinforce and strengthen the joint.
9. Lamanation of balsa wood members is not permitted.
10. Bridge cross members may not be closer than 2 cm to each other.

Write a reflection justifying why your bridge construction is the best model, using what you have learned in class and from your construction, and explain the practical uses of your bridge.

In this case, students may need scaffolding to come up with a design. Once again, a graphic organizer is helpful.

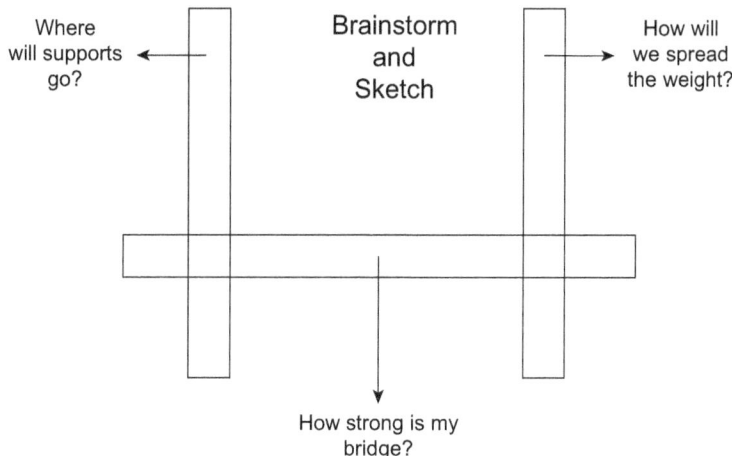

A Final Note

Scaffolding can encompass a wide range of strategies, including helping students learn to work together, participate in effective discourse, and activate their prior knowledge. We also need to model processes for students, use supportive questions without giving away the answer, and provide resources for students.

Points to Ponder

1. How will you use the information on students learning together and using discourse?
2. How might you improve your supportive questioning for students?
3. What resources do you need to provide for your students?
4. Which of the specific scaffolding strategies would you like to try?

Continue the Learning

Use the QR Code to access videos for your own use or for group professional development.

6

Assessment in the Productive Struggle Classroom

Once you have planned for productive struggle and implemented it, the natural question is how to assess it. We'll start by discussing the role of formative assessment, then move to discussing how to use formative assessment to measure the process of productive struggle and how to use summative assessment to measure the process.

Next, we'll turn our attention to options for using formative assessment to measure the content of productive struggle task, look at summative assessments to measure the content of productive struggle, and then talk about using rubrics to assess productive learning tasks.

Formative Assessment

Formative assessment is used periodically to check in with students and determine their understanding. It's designed for you to use it to inform your instruction and make appropriate adjustments, compared to summative assessment which provides summary information for grading. In this section, we'll be specifically addressing formative assessment for the process of productive struggle, and formative assessment for content.

Formative assessment, when used correctly, allows you to identify specific weaknesses for struggling students, and then gives you information on their progress. That's how you know what, how, and when to scaffold with your students. As you review the assessment strategies in this chapter, keep in mind the purpose is to improve your instruction and student learning. I prefer to use a teach-assess—then what flowchart.

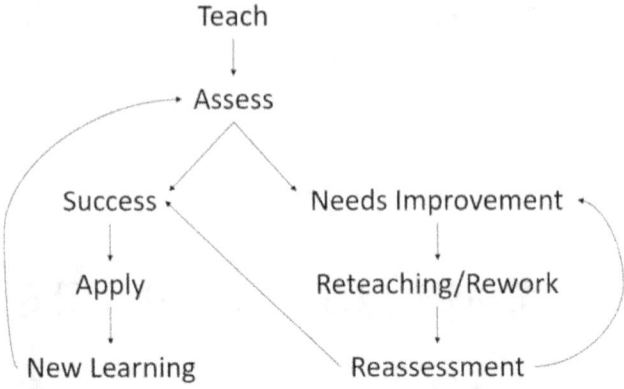

There are two broad ways to use formative assessment. First, you can assess individual student performance and use that information to help a particular student.

Forms for Formatively Assessing Individual Students

Individual Assessment	
Name	
What He/She Is Doing Well	What He/She Needs to Work On
What I Need To Do For This Student	

Class Roster			
Student	What They Are Doing Well	What They Need to Work On	Teacher's Next Step

Additionally, you can look at the overall picture of assessment for all students to understand patterns of performance. This can help you adjust your instruction for the class.

Patterns of Performance			
Use + if student mastered area, – if they are struggling, and 0 if they are totally stuck.			
Student's Name	Vocabulary	Understanding Connections	Facts and Content Mastery

(Continued)

Patterns of Performance

Use + if student mastered area, – if they are struggling, and 0 if they are totally stuck.

Student's Name	Vocabulary	Understanding Connections	Facts and Content Mastery

Pattern Analysis

Review individual assessment to pull patterns.

Pattern I Observed	My Next Steps

Assessing the Productive Struggle Process

Now let's look at a variety of engaging ways to assess the productive struggle process. You can easily adapt these to assess content if you prefer.

Observations

An important formative assessment tool for teachers is the use of observations. Observations can be planned, or they can be spontaneous. In an observation, you simply observe what students are doing, and take notes for documentation. You may choose to observe for productive struggle behaviors, or you may simply observe to see what happens from a general standpoint.

The most effective observations are planned. For example, if you want to see a student's problem-solving ability, you would schedule time to observe the student during the productive struggle task. The documentation, which may include simply taking notes, allows you to have a record of the student's skills at that point in time. By assessing it along with other formal and informal assessments, you gain a more accurate picture of the student's problem-solving abilities. You can also observe a student or a group. Also, it's important to note that during observations, you don't want to step in with a student. Rather, let them struggle and observe what is happening.

I've always found it helpful to use a template for observations.

Observation Template	
Student/Group	*Date*
Focus of Observation	
General Notes	
Strengths	*Weaknesses*
Next Steps	

This is a more structured alternative I've used in a group setting:

Group Observation Template

Group:

	Strengths	Challenges	Next Steps
Sticking with the task when it isn't easy			
Using graphic organizers and other tools when needed			
Asking for help when needed			

Checklists

Checklists are a strategy that can be used as a part of observations. Checklists can be simple yes/no tallies, or they can be open-ended for teachers to add notes.

Sample Mathematics Checklist

Characteristic	Notes
Student demonstrates problem-solving ability.	
Student demonstrates persistence while solving problems.	

| **Sample Mathematics Checklist** ||
Characteristic	Notes
Student reflects on his/her thinking.	
Student shows applications of learning in real life.	

| **Sample Cross-Curricular Checklist** ||
Characteristic	Notes
Student demonstrates persistence while writing.	
Student reflects throughout the process and uses metacognitive skills when appropriate.	
Student asks for help when needed, but only after struggling to solve problem himself/herself.	

Toolbox Check

A toolbox check can be used before students begin their productive struggle to assess if they have all their tools ready to use.

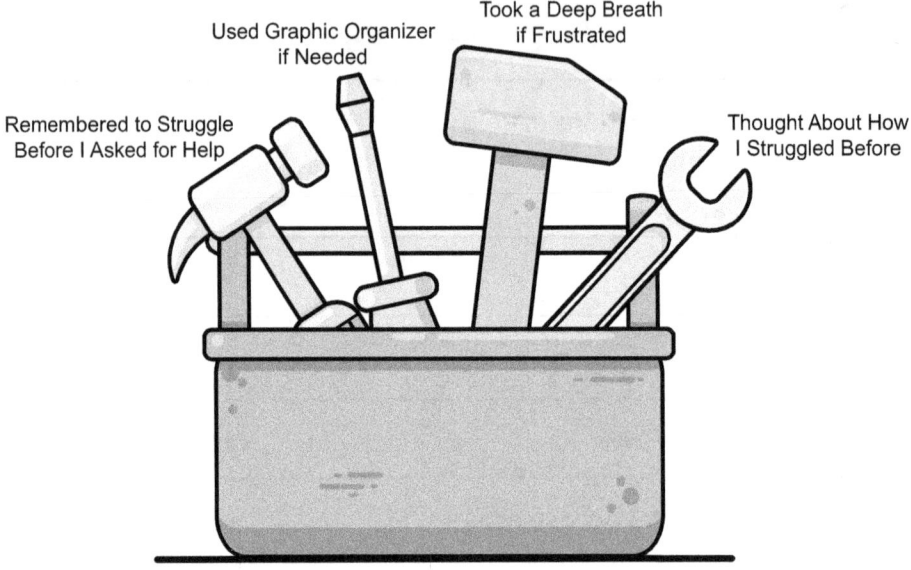

Mischievous Misconceptions

Throughout the productive struggle process, ask students to identify any misconceptions they have during the activity and what they learned that was correct. At the end, collect all the misconceptions and discuss them as a class.

Nudge Needed

Students have a small square that signifies they need a nudge or help while they are working.

Stoplight

Another creative way is to use a stoplight to reflect their productive struggle process. Green means "I'm moving fine," yellow means "I'm struggling in a good way," and red means "I'm stuck."

Two Squares

Using this option, students are given a paper square that is one color on side one, a different color on side two. Your school colors are one way to choose the colors. During the task or activity, you ask students to hold up their square: One color means Struggling in a Good Way; the other color is Struggling in a Bad Way. In a Social Studies classroom you can use a bill on one side (struggling and not making progress) and a law on the other (I've made progress). You can use anything here that provides two choices; just decide which represents the student is okay and which represents the student needs help. Here are some creative options.

Good vs. Bad Struggle	
Struggling in a Good Way	*Struggling in a Bad Way*
Phone Screen with a Thumbs Up	Phone Screen with a Thumbs Down
Lab Goggles Bright	Lab Goggles Dark
Theatre Mask Comedy	Theatre Mask Drama
Camera Open Lens	Camera Closed Lens
Whole Note Musical Note	Half Note Musical Note
Fully Inflated Tire	Flat Tire
Computer Screen with Picture	Computer Screen with Error Message
Hands Shaking	Fists Hitting
Microscope Slide Clear	Microscope Slide Dark
Open Book	Closed Book

Stick to It

Each time they stick with a problem after a setback, they note it in their log, keeping a comprehensive view of their perseverance.

	Stick to It	
	Date	When I Stuck with a Problem
☐		
☐		
☐		

Strategy Cards

Students are provided access to decks of strategy cards, cards that represent strategies they can use when they struggle. Samples include graphic organizers, drawing a picture, or asking what-if questions. Each time they use a strategy, they collect a card.

Uncertain Understandings

Students take note during the productive struggle process of times they were uncertain. As they continue the process, they note what they learned or how they became more certain.

Uncertain Understandings	
Uncertainty	How I Became More Certain

Rescue Request

Students draw or write to fill in a series of tweets showing "When I was stuck, I asked ___ for ___. Then . . ."

Rescue Request			
When I was stuck . . .	I asked . . .	For . . .	Then . . .

Weather Check-in

Part of productive struggle is how students feel while they are working. Using small cards, ask them to hold up a symbol that represents their feelings while working: sunny, cloudy, stormy, rainbow. Depending on their response, you may need to provide extra support, such as when they are stormy.

Summative Assessments for the Process of Productive Struggle

Now, let's look at strategies that you can do to assess the productive struggle process after they have completed the task or activity.

Checking My Toolbox Again

They can also revisit the toolbox after the activity to assess if or how they used the tools.

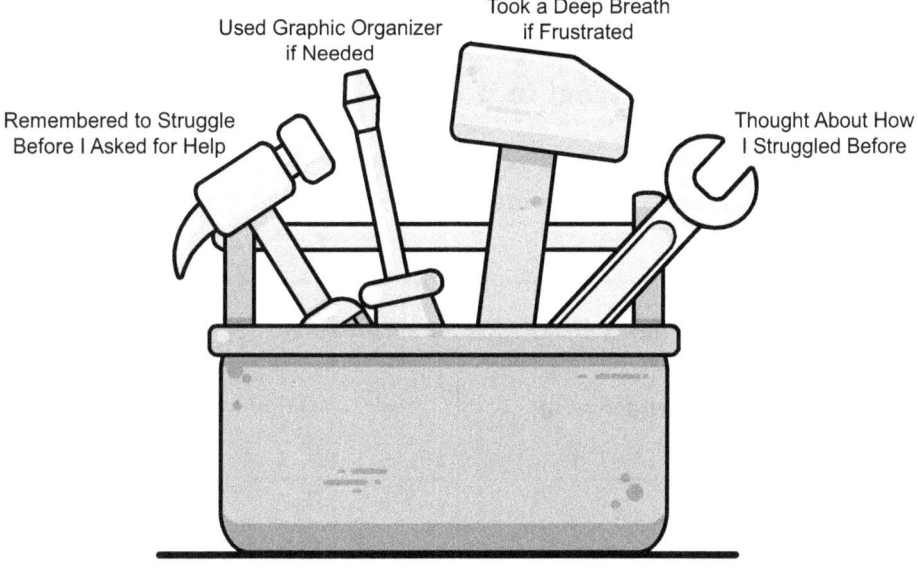

Sketch How You Are Doing (Up, Great, Down, Not So Good, etc.)

Ask students to sketch the ups and downs of their activity, similar to a graph. They go up when they do well, down when it isn't as good, and in the middle if things are flat. Since they complete this during the activity, you can check in with students as a formative assessment, but discussing the finished form allows you to get a summative picture of the process.

When I Didn't Know What to Do

Another option is to do a certificate/feedback form for students to complete. They start with: "When I didn't know what to do. . . ." and then complete "I did. . . ."

When I Didn't Know What to Do . . .	
When I didn't know what to do . . .	*Then I did . . .*

Roses and Thorns

Another option is to use a rose metaphor. They identify thorns (things that stuck them) and then the flower is how they overcame them or succeeded.

Think Like a . . .

Ask students to reflect on the productive struggle task from the particular of a particular role related to the task. Then, they do a two minute video as to how they completed the task, using the chosen perspective.

"Think Like A" Roles

Author
Writer
Scientist
Historian
Mathematician

Peer Observations

Students keep a peer observation log for their group, noting anytime their peers demonstrate the observation area.

	Peer Observations		
Observation Area	*Peer One*	*Peer Two*	*Peer Three*
Shows curiosity and creative thinking			
Shows persistence			
Shows problem-solving			
Takes risks			
Integrates learning with other topics, books, subjects, or real life			

I'm Climbing Up

Use a mountain graphic, ask students to mark their progress.

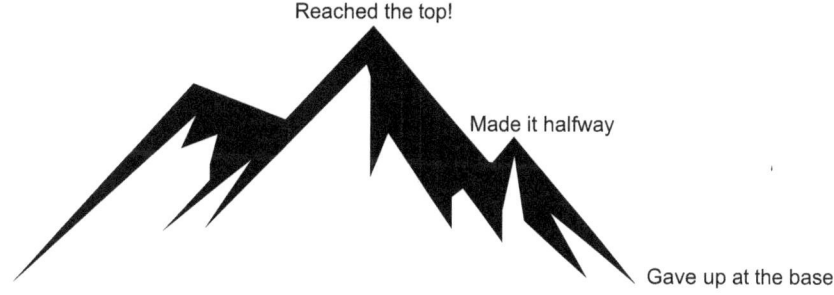

Assess Athletic Performance

Students use athletic roles to assess their overall performance.

- **Rookie:** Just starting, need lots of help.
- **Starter:** Can handle the basics, but need support.
- **Playmaker:** Confident and consistent in my performance.
- **Coach:** Can explain it and help others.

Evaluating My Entrepreneurial Spirit

Alternatively, students can use entrepreneurial roles for assessment.

- **Explorer:** Just starting out, figuring out where to go.
- **Builder:** Progressing, can do some parts on my own.
- **Connector:** Confident with concepts, making links to other learning.
- **Innovator:** Expert in learning, can apply in new ways and help others.

Emoji Emotions

Students slide a clip or sticker along a range of emojis to reflect on how they managed their emotions while productively struggling.

Frustration   Confused   Thinking   Okay   Happy   Excited

Checking in on Teamwork

We looked at this rubric in Chapter 3, but let's revisit it as a summative assessment. Students can use the rubric to self-assess, or you can use it to assess how well students worked in teams.

	Collaborative Learning Rubric		
	You're a Team Player!	*You're Working On It . . .*	*You're Flying Solo*
G Group dedication	The student is totally dedicated to his or her group, offering all of his or her attention by actively listening to peers and responding with ideas.	The student is partially dedicated to his or her group though sometimes becomes distracted by students or issues outside the group.	The student spends most of his or her time focusing on things outside of the group; he or she is not available for discussion or group work.

Collaborative Learning Rubric

	You're a Team Player!	*You're Working On It...*	*You're Flying Solo*
R Responsibility	The student shares responsibility equally with other group members and accepts his or her role in the group.	The student takes on responsibility but does not completely fulfill his or her obligations.	The student either tries to take over the group and does not share responsibilities or takes no part at all in the group work assigned.
O Open communication	The student gives polite and constructive criticism to group members when necessary, welcomes feedback from peers, resolves conflict peacefully, and asks questions when a group goal is unclear.	The student gives criticism, though often in a blunt manner, reluctantly accepts criticism from peers, and may not resolve conflict peacefully all of the time.	The student is quick to point out the faults of other group members yet is unwilling to take any criticism in return; often the student argues with peers rather than calmly coming to a consensus.
U Utilization of work time	The student is always on task, working with group members to achieve goals, objectives, and deadlines.	The student is on task most of the time but occasionally takes time off from working with the group.	The student does not pay attention to the task at hand and frustrates other group members because of his or her inability to complete work in a timely fashion.

(Continued)

Collaborative Learning Rubric			
	You're a Team Player!	*You're Working On It . . .*	*You're Flying Solo*
P Participation	The student is observed sharing ideas, reporting research findings to the group, taking notes from other members, and offering assistance to his or her peers as needed.	The student sometimes shares ideas or reports findings openly but rarely takes notes from other group members.	The student does not openly share ideas or findings with the group, and neither does he or she take notes on peers' ideas.

Overall Summary of Productive Struggle

If you want an overall picture of their productive struggle from the student's standpoint, you might use a formal self-assessment.

Self-Assessment of Productive Struggle		
	Rank Yourself from 1–5	*Evidence for Ranking*
I felt positive about my learning.		
When I struggled, I demonstrated perseverance.		
When I was stuck, I tried alternative ways of learning.		

Self-Assessment of Productive Struggle		
	Rank Yourself from 1–5	*Evidence for Ranking*
If I truly needed it, I asked for help.		
I used a variety of strategies and tools to help me learn.		

You can also use a more open-ended approach.

Finish the Sentence Self-assessment of Productive Struggle

> In today's lesson, I learned . . .
> In today's lesson, I thought . . .
> In today's lesson, I felt . . .
> Something I'm proud of is . . .
> Something I'd do differently is . . .

Beginner's Rubric for Productive Struggle

Finally, you can use the following rubric to assess individual students, assess groups of students, or allow them to self-assess progress for themselves or their group, using the five dispositions from Chapter 2.

Student Dispositions Rubric			
Category	*Beginning*	*Developing*	*Proficient*
Curiosity	Shows little interest in something new or asking questions.	When prompted, student asks questions or shows interest in something new.	Regularly asks thoughtful questions and often explores new ideas.
Persistence	Quits when student isn't successful.	Is willing to try again if teacher encourages him or her.	Doesn't give up on the first try and regularly tries again.
Problem-Solving	Struggles with complex problems and typically only tries one strategy.	With guidance, student will struggle to solve complex problems and try alternatives.	Student works independently to solve complex problems and will try alternatives.
Taking Risks	Student works on easy tasks and does not like to try new things.	With guidance, student tries new things. With encouragement, will try again after making mistake.	Student tries challenging tasks independently and works through mistakes.
Making Connections	Does not connect learning to real life or other subjects.	Makes some connections to other subjects or real life.	Regularly connects ideas across subjects and to real-life experiences.

Now, let's turn our attention to formative and summative strategies for assessing the content during the productive struggle process.

Formatively Assessing the Content During the Process

Build-a-Meme

At some point during the learning, ask students to stop and create a meme for Instagram about their learning.

Illustrate Connections

Ask students to draw the connections they have made during the lesson so far.

Around the Circle (Each Person Says One Thing, Keep Going)

If students are working in groups, go around in a circle and ask each person to say one thing they have learned and one question they still have.

What's the Big Picture?

Ask students to share "the big picture." In other words, they share a real-life connection they have made during their learning.

Explain It to Someone

Imagine you are a famous person or character related to the task. Ask students to explain what they are learning to your person/character.

SOS

Students write or draw a quick summary, their opinion about what they have learned, and support or evidence for their opinion.

Word Cloud Generator

Ask students to use vocabulary from their task to create a word cloud. They can do this manually or with a free online tool.

Pipe Cleaner/Craft Stick

Students use a fuzzy craft stick to create a shape that represents their learning. Then, they explain why the shape demonstrates their learning.

"Short" Summary

Students create a "short" video suitable for TikTok or Instagram that summarizes their learning.

Make It New

Make it New allows you to see if students can apply their learning. Students choose an image: a book, a face, the earth, or an exclamation point. Then, they write how what they have learned applies to another book/text they have read, themselves, the real world, or something else.

Make It New			
How it applies to another book/text	*How it applies to me*	*How it applies to the real world*	*How it applies to something else*

You've Got Mail

In one of their blogs, Edutopia (www.edutopia.org/resource/checking-understanding-download) recommends using "You've Got Mail." As the author describes it,

> Each student writes a question about a topic on the front of an envelope; the answer is included inside. Questions are then "mailed" around the room. Each learner writes his or her answer on a slip of scratch paper and confirms its correctness by reading the "official answer" before placing his or her own response in the envelope. After several series of mailings and a class discussion about the subject, the envelopes are deposited in the teacher's letterbox.

Wall of Knowledge

Angela Stockman, on the blog brilliant-insane.com, describes "Add a Brick to the Wall of Knowledge." She recommends creating a bulletin board, and giving students paper bricks. Ask them to write about what they have learned, and place (or staple) their bricks on the wall throughout the year. You could also give students boxes, and they could write new learning on the different sides of the box. Stack the boxes together to create a wall.

Bounce the Ball

In Bounce the Ball, use a beach ball to assess what students know. The first student makes a point about the lesson. Then, they throw the ball to another student who either expands on the first point, asks a question, or makes another point. The game continues until students run out of points.

Always-Sometimes-Never True

In Always-Sometimes-Never True, the teacher makes a statement that could meet any of the three options. Then, students move to the front, middle, or back of the room to discuss their choice. Finally, the teacher leads a whole-group discussion. This is particularly helpful when there is not a yes or no choice.

Summative Assessment of the Content

To summatively assess the content of the productive struggle lesson, you want to focus on two characteristics.

Accurately measures what the students learned

Decide the level of struggle for the assessment

First, be sure the type of summative assessment accurately measures what the students learned. For example, if students created a project, the project itself can be the summative assessment. However, you may also want to use a short answer or essay question so that students can reflect of their learning. Alternatively, should you want to measure knowledge of facts, true-false, matching, or multiple choice tests may be appropriate.

Next, decide if you want an element of struggle in the summative assessment or if you want it to be written at an easier level. Realistically, that is up to you. I prefer to still have a level of challenge in my assessments, but you may not want that. I'll be giving you options for more challenge should you want to use them.

Traditional Types of Summative Assessment

> Matching Tests
> True-False Tests
> Multiple-Choice Tests
> Short Answer Questions
> Essay Questions

Matching Tests

Matching tests are an easy, quick way to assess a wide range of student knowledge. However, it is difficult to assess at a higher level of challenge, as most matching tests measure basic recall questions. Depending on the items, students can guess rather than truly demonstrate understanding.

What are the best strategies for developing quality matching tests? First, make sure there is one best option for each item you list. Ensure that students can see why the items match so there is clear evidence students understand the link. Also, provide more examples than matching items. For example, if you have a list of vocabulary terms and then definitions, add one or two extra definitions to increase the challenge.

Another option to increase challenge is to use a three-column matching test. With this choice, students must understand three levels of content rather than two.

Three-Column Matching Test		
Biome	*Description*	*Example*

True-False Tests

True-false tests are an excellent way for students to determine the accuracy of a statement, agree with opinions, and define terms. As with matching items, they are graded quickly and easily, and students can answer a wide range of questions in a short amount of time. However, once again, questions are typically low-level recall questions, and you may not be sure students understand the question or if they are simply guessing. To combat this and to increase the challenge, require students to rewrite any false choices as true statements, which does require them to demonstrate a true understanding of the content.

Multiple-Choice Tests

Multiple-choice tests are probably the most commonly used tests in classrooms across the nation, and they have several benefits. Although due in part to preparation for standardized tests, they are also easy to score. They also apply to a wide range of cognitive skills, including higher-order-thinking ones. Finally, incorrect answers, if written and explained correctly, can help you diagnose a student's problem areas. Disadvantages include that the questions can't measure a student's ability to create or synthesize information and that students can guess an answer.

There are three ways to write multiple-choice questions that allow you to increase the challenge. First, choose a question that moves beyond basic recall. Next, create choices for the stem that are clearly correct or incorrect without making them too easy. In other words, if we provide examples that are clearly off topic, it makes it easier for students to guess. Finally, although some teachers do not like to use "all of the above," "none of the above," "a and d" options, or "mark all of the above," we do find they require students to think at a higher level than basic recall. Remember, you know your students; adapt the suggestions so they match your students' needs.

Short-Answer Questions

Short-answer questions are an expanded form of fill in the blank. Responses are not as long as essays, but they usually include more than one sentence. Because students are required to create a response, they are more challenging than the types of items we've already discussed. You'll need to build challenge into the context of your questions, asking questions that require more than just a list. Although more challenging to grade than matching, true-false, fill-in-the-blank, and multiple-choice questions, they are simpler than assessing essay questions.

Essay Questions

Essay questions are one of the most common assessments used in today's classrooms. Essay questions are extremely effective for measuring complex learning. Opportunities for guessing are removed, so you can truly measure what students understand. There are several disadvantages, including the amount of time to grade them, the subjective nature of grading and the dependency of the answer on the student's writing ability.

When you are writing essay questions, crafting the question is particularly important. You want to be sure the complexity of the learning outcome is reflected in a clear, focused manner. It's also important to provide explicit instructions as to your expectations.

> Explain what you wanted to discover with your investigation. How did your investigation answer the question? Provide evidence from your investigation to support your opinion.

Performance-Based Assessment

Performance-based assessments are a type of summative assessments, but they differ from traditional testing. They are focused on students performing in some manner to demonstrate their understanding. Typically, performance-based assessments are more challenging, because students must go in depth to complete the performance, project, or portfolio. Many of the productive struggle tasks and activities provided throughout the book were examples of performance-based assessments.

Using Rubrics for Summative Assessment

Particularly when using performance-based tasks and assessments, rubrics are helpful. They assist students in understanding the task, and they help teachers with grading.

How do you develop a rubric? First, decide on the categories that you will be assessing, as well as a scale for scoring. Then, write the indicators for each category and score. I'd add a caution here—too often, we base our scoring on quantity (includes 1 reason vs. 3 reasons) when we really want quality. Keep that in mind with your descriptors. Finally, share the rubric with your students and gather feedback. This way you can ensure the rubric accurately measures what you want. You can even create it together with your students. Here's a sample you can use when students are presenting information.

Presentation Rubric (Middle/High School)			
Category	*Finding My Voice*	*Owning the Stage*	*Commanding the Spotlight*
Content and Ideas	Ideas are unclear or incomplete; limited understanding shown.	Ideas are mostly clear; shows understanding with some supporting detail.	Ideas are insightful, accurate, and well-supported with evidence or examples.
Organization and Flow	Presentation is hard to follow; missing clear intro or conclusion.	Organized with a beginning, middle, and end; transitions are sometimes smooth.	Clear, logical flow with strong opening, smooth transitions, and powerful conclusion.
Delivery (Voice, Eye Contact, Body Language)	Speaks too softly or quickly; little eye contact; body language distracts.	Speaks clearly most of the time; some eye contact; body language generally supports the message.	Speaks with confidence and expression; maintains strong eye contact; body language enhances the message.

(Continued)

Presentation Rubric (Middle/High School)			
Category	*Finding My Voice*	*Owning the Stage*	*Commanding the Spotlight*
Visuals/Media	Visuals are messy, missing, or distract from the message.	Visuals are mostly clear, neat, and connected to the presentation.	Visuals are polished, creative, and strongly reinforce the message.
Audience Engagement	Limited attempt to engage; audience loses interest.	Some effort to engage audience through questions, tone, or interaction.	Keeps audience engaged throughout with energy, interaction, and strong presence.

Now, let's go back to one of our examples from earlier in the book.

> You are a scientist researching new vaccines to combat viruses in our society. Research the benefits and disadvantages on all stakeholders, including analyzing biases that exist. Then, create a proposed set of vaccine development guidelines to send to the CDC that are justified by scientific evidence rather than opinion.

Here's a sample rubric to use with students.

Vaccine Research and Guidelines Rubric

Criteria	Beginning	Developing	Mastering
Stakeholder Understanding	Identifies few or no stakeholders. Missing key stakeholders.	Although some stakeholders are included, the key information related to the stakeholders is shortchanged.	All major stakeholders are described, including their interests and constraints.
Evidence Quality and Use	General resources are used, typically at a surface level.	A mix of credible and surface information is used with only a short explanation of why sources are credible.	In depth, high-quality, evidence-based sources are used, work shows strength/limitations of evidence.
Bias Recognition and Analysis	Vague, limited addressing of bias.	Basic, surface addressing of bias.	Thorough analysis of bias also describes their impact on conclusions.
Counterarguments and Limitations	Does not address opposing views.	Insufficiently addresses opposing views.	Thoroughly addresses opposing views and responds with evidence-based points.
Original Insight and Synthesis	Summarizes rather than synthesizes information. No original insight.	Limited synthesis with minimal insight from the student.	Thorough synthesis incorporates many points of original thought.

Online sources such as Rubistar and iRubric, as well as many AI tools, can help you build rubrics. What I would recommend is, especially with AI, that you give very specific instructions, such as focusing on quality, not quantity. That's how I co-developed the vaccine rubric, and you can see how the descriptors are much stronger. It's also worth a google search to see if there is an existing rubric you might use or adapt.

A Final Note

Formative assessment for both the process and content of productive struggle can assist with improving instruction. It can also support your scaffolding. Additionally, it's important to use summative assessment for how students do productive struggle (the process) and the content of the productive struggle task. Using a variety of strategies for both formative and summative assessment will ensure you can positively impact student learning.

Points to Ponder

1. What formative process strategy would you like to try?
2. What formative product strategy would you like to try?
3. What summative process strategy would you like to try?
4. What summative product strategy would you like to try?

Continue the Learning

Use the QR Code to access videos for your own use or for group professional development.

7
Common Concerns About Productive Struggle

In this chapter, I'd like to address four questions that teachers commonly ask me about productive struggle.

> How should I address productive struggle with students with special needs?
>
> How do I address students who won't try?
>
> How do I communicate with parents and families about productive struggle?
>
> It seems to take a lot of time to plan and implement productive struggle in my classroom. I'm overwhelmed. What can I do?

How Should I Address Productive Struggle With Students With Special Needs?

This is a critical issue with productive struggle. When determining and using activities for students with special needs, the first consideration is the IEP. The Individualized Education Plan is a legal document that ensures students' specialized needs are met. It specified any accommodations and/or modifications you must provide to a student. In our book, *Rigor for Students with Special Needs, 2nd edition,* Brad Witzel and I provided an overview of modifications and accommodations.

Accommodations

Accommodations are changes that can be made to the way students with disabilities are instructed and assessed. The changes can be made to instructional methods and materials, assignments and assessments, learning environment, time demands and schedules, and/or special communication systems.

When deciding on the appropriate accommodation, consider the following questions:

Student Accommodation Considerations			
Step	*Consideration*	*Question*	*Response per Student*
1	Access	Does the student have an impairment that restricts access to the skill being assigned or tested?	
2	Availability	What accommodations (if any) are aligned with the impairment and available to provide access?	
3	Target	Will the accommodation maintain the construct being assigned or tested?	

Source: adapted from Kettler, (2012)

Modifications

Modifications are changes to what a student is expected to learn. In other words, the standard or concept is changed from general education expectations. Content modifications likely change what the test measures (McDonnell et al., 1997). Modifications, for example, may include deleting certain items that are inappropriate for an examinee or making constructed-response questions into multiple-choice questions. These types of modifications are presumed to change the nature of what is being tested. For standardized assessments, safeguards exist to secure that the construct of the question will not be altered or modified. Thus, the more modifications given to a student during their learning, the less likely that they will be prepared for an unmodified assessment.

Sample Accommodations and Modifications

Your state and/or school district may have an approved list of accommodations and modifications, but here are a few of the most common ones.

Sample Accommodations and Modifications	
Potential Accommodations	*Potential Modifications*
Presentation • Written directions, rather than only oral • Written or guided notes to go with lecture • Chunked lesson in small increments • Increased volume • Increased text size	Assessment • Different content • Different questions • Different responses required • Excuse from the assessment • Tools to answer standards-focused questions (e.g. dictionary for vocabulary or calculator for computational fluency)
Response • Dictation software for written assignments • Shortened assignments with same content • Spellcheck or dictionary, unless vocabulary/spelling objective • Chunked assignment in smaller increments	Assignment • Different project • Eliminated part of a project • Different questions • Eliminated questions • Different responses required • Tools to answer standards-focused questions (i.e. dictionary for vocabulary or calculator for computational fluency)

(Continued)

Sample Accommodations and Modifications

Potential Accommodations	Potential Modifications
Timing • Increased time to complete test or assignment • Increased wait time • Frequent breaks/chunked assignment or test	Curriculum • Different or eliminated standards • Different grading
Setting • Reduced distraction environment • Use of sensory tool for attention and focus • Preferable seating location • Different lighting	
Scheduling • Increased time to move between classes • Tests given a specific time of the day	
Organization • Visual timer and scheduler • Use of a planner, checked by teachers • More frequent assignment reminders • Additional assignment clarification • Weekly progress report	

Source: adapted from https://www.understood.org/en/learning-thinking-differences/treatments-approaches/educational-strategies/common-classroom-accommodations-and-modifications

The IEP is only the first step. You'll also want to consider what you know about the student in order to best meet his or her needs. Think of it this way—the IEP is the floor, not the ceiling. Use it to ensure success, but don't let it limit a student. I've found charting out information to be helpful when planning and using my assessments.

Assessment Form	
Based on the IEP and/or my pre-assessment data, what do I need to do with this student?	
My formative assessment plan	Modifications and accommodations needed based on the formative assessment
Summative assessment	Modifications and accommodations in the summative assessment

How Do I Address Students Who Won't Try?

Repeated failures and low achievement associated with learning disabilities often lead students to attribute their failures to internal causes and successes to external causes such as luck or ease of the task (Dweck & Elliott, 1983; Settle & Milich, 1999). When this is repeated over years, students develop a learned helplessness, knowing that they will fail, despite even good scores on tests and assignments. Therefore, it is fair to conclude that students with a history of academic failure develop learned helplessness.

Learned helplessness is a process of conditioning where student seek help from others even when they have mastered information. See if this example looks familiar:

> A student is asked to solve a direct reading comprehension problem, but he immediately raises his hand. When the teacher comes

over, the student says he needs help. So the teacher reads the paragraph to the student and re-explains the question. The student still doesn't answer the question. Next, the teacher re-explains a regularly used comprehension strategy with the student. Finally, the teacher walks through the strategy and may even solve the problem for the student.

While this scenario sounds justifiable, and maybe even familiar, the teacher is reinforcing the student's learned helplessness. This exchange undermines the student's independent ability to solve the problem. Such exchanges that continue a student's learned helplessness include an increased time of completion, lack of academic perseverance, refusal to initiate an attempt, or general off-task behavior. Thus, once a student has begun a run of learned helplessness, expect to see the outcomes repeatedly. In the previous scenario, the student must learn to attend to the teacher's group instruction and attempt to solve problems.

Instead of running to the rescue of students who can succeed without us or even refuse to help such students, it is important to find ways to teach students to gain independence in their problem-solving. In other words, find out why the student is behaving in a certain way and plan a response that best builds academic success and independence. One way to help is to teach students how to learn and succeed without instantly making excuses and asking for help by following these steps.

1. Determine if learned helplessness exists
2. Explicitly model the student the preferred academic behavior
3. Teach the student a strategy for displaying the preferred academic behavior
4. Provide practice for the strategy
5. Set a cue to remind the student to initiate the strategy
6. Allow the student to succeed
7. Facilitate the student's problem solving strategy

There are other strategies that can help with learned helplessness. These include normalizing mistakes so they are more willing to try, reframing mistakes so students see them as opportunities, setting achievable goals so they do not see the task as overwhelming, and providing choice when possible.

How Do I Communicate With Parents and Families About Productive Struggle?

There are three ways to communicate with parents and families.

> Communication to Parents and Families
> Communication from Parents and Families
> Communication With Parents and Families

Communication to Parents and Families

When I talk to parents, many of them feel as though there is a hidden code in schools; a code they don't understand. Margo and her son moved to a new area when Jared started middle school. She missed the first parent-teacher meeting because she was working. She called the school and left several messages asking to meet with his teacher but didn't receive a return call. Margo was frustrated when she told me her story. Another teacher at the school was in one of my classes, so I talked with her. I discovered that the school had a policy that all appointments with teachers were scheduled with the attendance secretary so that times could be coordinated with all teachers on the team. My graduate student said the principal always explained the policy at the first meeting. So, of course, Margo didn't know because she wasn't at the meeting, and she thought the teacher was just ignoring her. One phone call later, she connected with the teacher, and she and Jared finished the year successfully.

I recommend you have a one page fact sheet about productive struggle in your classroom. By clearly describing what you are doing, parents are more likely to understand what is happening. In addition to making it accessible to parents and families through your website, remind families of critical aspects through social media postings and newsletters.

> ### *Productive Struggle One Page Fact Sheet*
>
> *What Is Productive Struggle?*
> Productive struggle is the process of students grappling with a challenging task, making mistakes, and continuing to persist in order to build deeper learning.

Why Are We Using Productive Struggle?

We want all our students to learn at higher levels rather than just doing easy work. We want them to use problem-solving skills and learn life skills such as persistence and independence.

Important Facts

- When students work at levels that do not require struggle, they do not necessarily make progress.
- Learning to persist through struggle is a life skill for students and also helps them become more independent and confident learners.
- When students struggle and continue to learn, they learn at higher levels.

What You'll See With Your Student

There will be times he or she will asked to work individually or in groups on tasks that are challenging. These will be tasks that are not too easy and not impossible, but they are ones your son or daughter will find challenging. Ahead of time, teachers will model what students are expected to do, and they will teach students ways to help themselves during the activity. Teachers are also available for help, but will encourage students to try themselves before they ask for help.

What You Can Do

When your son or daughter is struggling, encourage him or her to continue to work, and to use the strategies the teacher has provided. Don't do the work for them—that's the worst thing you can do. Ask lots of questions that can help your student, such as "How have you handled this before?" or "How can you figure this out on your own?"

For More Information

Contact your student's teacher for more assistance.

I spoke with one teacher about providing information to families. A parent asked her about how she could support her son when he was struggling. She had a simple response.

> A part of productive struggle is grit, which is sticking with something important to you even when it's hard, boring, or takes time according to Angela Duckworth. Grit is important because it can help predict long term success and it helps develop resilience. As your student is working with productive struggle, you can encourage grit by modeling your own perseverance, praise effort, not just results, and remind them that failure is a part of learning.

Keeping it simple, yet clear is helpful.

Additionally, whenever students are working on a productive struggle project, make those expectations clear not only to students, but to parents in writing. One of my principals always reminded me, "The worst thing you can hear from a parent is 'If I had only known.'" Your goal is no surprises!

Communication From Parents and Families

It's also important to have communication from parents and families. There will be times that you need information from them in order to best meet the needs of your students. I remember talking to a neighbor a few years ago. She had received multiple calls and emails from the school, but had not returned them. She was worried they wanted to give her bad news. I convinced her to call her son's science teacher. The teacher was simply concerned because her son's performance was deteriorating. The teacher wanted to help, but wondered if anything was happening at home. My neighbor explained that her ex-husband was remarrying, and her son was unsure as to what that would mean to him. The teacher was empathetic, and assured my neighbor she would provide extra help at school to ensure his success. My neighbor was relieved to know of the additional support, and the teacher was able to provide that support since she knew the situation.

I like to periodically ask parents and family members for key information.

Feedback Form	
How do you think your son/daughter is doing in school?	
Is there anything you are concerned about?	
What can I do to help your son/daughter?	
Is there anything else I should know?	

Communication With Parents and Families

Finally, there is communication with parents and families. This is the highest level of communication, representing a true back-and-forth in which, together, you make decisions about a student.

There are 10 keys to effective communication that are helpful.

> **10 Principles of Effective Communication**
> Conciseness and consistency matter
> Open with your key point
> Match to your agenda
> Make it coherent
> Understand your audience
> Name your objective/desired action
> Courtesy rules
> Ask questions
> Tell a story
> Empathy helps

Using these keys can help you develop a true partnership. Although you'll want to consider them anytime you are communicating, they are especially helpful during conferences. Keep these in mind as you review my five steps for a GREAT parent/family conference.

Good news is the way to start!

Relate your opinion so they understand you want to help their child.

Evidence is provided to support your opinion.

Accept their perspective as valid.

Thought-provoking questions help all participants share.

It's our responsibility to connect with parents and families; and the benefits outweigh any costs in terms of time.

It Seems to Take a Lot of Time to Plan and Implement Productive Struggle in My Classroom. I'm Overwhelmed. What Can I Do?

Managing all aspects of productive struggle can be overwhelming. Staying organized is a key aspect of using productive struggle effectively. I've found there are 3 key strategies that can help.

Streamline the Process

Organize Your Files

Collect Your Key Resources

Streamline the Process

First, streamline what you do. You want to be effective, but you don't want to have so many choices that it overwhelms you. For example, I visited a kindergarten teacher one day. She regularly used K-W-Ls for pre-assessment, which is a great tool. However, she opened a file drawer and showed me almost 200 patterns for K-W-Ls—one for each day of the year. That's great—but you don't need that. If you want some variety in the look of a graphic organizer, have a few, but don't go overboard.

In another situation, a teacher shared with me her coding for feedback on student work. She had been writing out every comment on every paper. She realized that, for the most part, she used 7–10 general comments. She developed a code for those, taught it to students and families, and was able to save about 60% of her grading time by using the code. She could then focus on comments at the end or in a unique situation.

Organize Your Files

Another important aspect of managing assessment is to organize your files. You can do this with paper or electronically. Start with the basics. Build a folder for general pre-assessments, one for productive struggle formative assessments, then one for productive struggle summative assessments. You'll put generic options here that you can pull for use at any time.

Next, move to specific subjects if you teach more than one. Build similar folders that work just for that content area. Third, and this is most critical, build folders for each unit or topic you teach and organize the tasks, formative assessments, and summative assessments. This is your go-to set of folders next year when you are teaching the same topic. Don't be overwhelmed with this—just organize as you go through the year, and then you'll have it done. Again, it's up to you whether you organize with paper or electronically. Choose what works best for you.

Collect Your Key Resources

Finally, you probably have some key productive struggle resources that you regularly access. It's time to organize those too! I use two electronic methods for this, but you can also do it with printouts. First, I bookmark all my key resources in a folder called productive struggle. If you want to be super organized, you can have subfolders here for rubrics, tasks, graphic organizers, etc.

I also keep an email folder for productive struggle. These are emails I receive that contain resources I want to review later. When I have time, I read the information and bookmark as necessary.

A Final Note

When incorporating productive struggle in your classroom, you may face particular challenges. Addressing students with special needs, working with those who won't try, communicating with parents, and finding time to plan are important issues to deal with.

Points to Ponder

1. What strategy can help you work with students with special needs?
2. How can you address learned helplessness in your situation?
3. How would you like to communicate with parents about productive struggle?
4. What tip on finding and managing time would you like to try?

Continue the Learning

Use the QR Code to access videos for your own use or for group professional development.

8

Collaborating for Productive Struggle

One of the things we have learned as educators is that working together makes us more effective. This is particularly true when we are trying to improve our instruction in productive struggle. Many teachers are members of professional learning communities.

The original meaning of a professional community of learners reflected the commitment of teachers and leaders who continuously seek to grow professionally and act upon their new learning. Learning communities are focused on student learning. Teachers who belong to a learning community want to improve their classroom instruction. In this chapter, we'll focus on three areas related to collaboration and learning communities.

> How Can I Find Time to Work With Other Teachers?
> What Does Collaboration Look Like?
> Activities for Professional Learning Communities

How Can I Find Time to Work With Other Teachers?

It is important that teachers have time to work with colleagues on professional tasks. This collaborative time is one of the catalysts for nurturing and sustaining change. Teachers value the opportunity to meet with grade or content peers to discuss successes, diagnose ways to improve, develop a repertoire of strategies that they can use in their own classrooms, and provide critical input to school improvement plans.

There are many different ways to provide collaborative time and they vary considerably depending on the grade level of the school. Unfortunately, most of these options are not controlled by teachers. I share them so that you can consider options to discuss with your leadership team. These samples are from Ronald Williamson in our leadership book, *7 Strategies for School Improvement*.

Ways to Provide Collaborative Time	
Common Planning	When teachers share a common planning period some of the time may be used for collaborative work.
Parallel Scheduling	When special teachers (physical education, music, art, etc.) are scheduled so that grade level or content area teachers have common planning.
Shared Classes	Teachers in more than one grade or team combine their students into a single large class for specific instruction and the other teachers can collaborate.
Faculty Meeting	Find other ways to communicate the routine items shared during faculty meetings and reallocate that time to collaborative activities.
Adjust Start or End of Day	Members of a team, grade, or entire school agree to start their workday early or extend their workday one day a week to gain collaborative time.
Late Start or Early Release	Adjust the start or end of the school day for students and use the time for collaborative activity.
Professional Development Days	Rather than traditional large group professional development use the time for teams of teachers to engage in collaborative work.

Angela Evans, the Instructional Dean at Tulsa Technology Center shared how her school provides collaborative time. They developed a "released time" schedule that allows every teacher to work with other teachers on instructional issues. The deans organize the schedule to provide two days during the year for this important work.

Regardless of the way you provide time for collaboration, the most important thing is how the time is used. It is important that it be productive and supports your school's vision, and only the participants can control that.

What Does Collaboration Look Like?

In *The Essential Guide to Professional Learning: Collaboration*, the Australian Institute for Teaching and School Leadership points out there is an important difference between collaboration, which is the goal of Professional Learning Communities, and cooperation.

Collaboration vs. Cooperation	
Collaboration "to work with another or others on a joint project"	*Cooperation* "to be of assistance or willing to help"
Joint planning, decision-making, and problem-solving Job embedded and long term Formal and informal Common goals High levels of trust	Individual ownership of goals with others providing assistance for mutual benefit Resources and materials are shared as required Often spontaneous arrangements Passive engagement by others Often short term No set structure or arrangements

Notice the differences between the two. It's a bit like putting two pens beside each other vs. using a pen with four colors inside it. Do you truly work together?

Activities for Professional Learning Communities

Although there are many ways for teachers to work together, we are going to take a look at 7 of the most common.

> ### Seven Activities for Professional Learning Communities
>
> A Parade of Productive Struggle: Sharing My Lesson
>
> Playback for Progress: Video Observations of Productive Struggle
>
> Peeking with Purpose: Visiting Classrooms to see Productive Struggle
>
> "I Spy" for Patterns with Productive Struggle
>
> Learning in Action Through Lesson Studies
>
> Looking at the How: Developing Consistent Expectations for the Process of Productive Struggle
>
> Looking at Student Work: Developing Consistent Expectations for the Products of Productive Struggle

A Parade of Productive Struggle: Sharing My Lesson

One way you can work together as a small or large group of teachers is to have a Lesson Plan Parade. Ask each teacher to share a lesson plan with productive struggle and post it on the wall around the room. Teachers "read the room" and post ribbons with a positive statement about each lesson plan. This works well as a springboard for planning additional productive struggle lessons.

Playback for Progress:
Video Observations of Productive Struggle

Another option to improve your productive struggle instruction is to watch other lessons. You may find some online, or teachers can take turns videoing a lesson in their class. What's key is looking at all aspects of the lesson.

Video Viewing Guide	
Productive Struggle Focus	
What Happened Before Productive Struggle to Enhance Student Success	
Instruction for the Process	Instruction for the Content
What I Noticed During Productive Struggle	
About the Process	About the Content
What I Noticed After the Productive Struggle	
Successes I Want to Share	Challenges I Want to Discuss

Over time, you will begin to notice patterns you see in multiple lessons, which can help everyone improve their instruction.

Peeking With Purpose: Visiting Classrooms to See Productive Struggle

If you are able to physically visit classrooms, that is an ideal way to learn about productive struggle. I've found at the middle/high school level, it works well to visit other grade levels, since teachers at the same grade level typically have planning at the same time. Ideally, you can discuss the lesson with the teacher to be observed in advance and receive a lesson plan or outline so you know what you will be seeing. You can use the video guide from earlier, or the alternate provided next.

Peeking With Purpose Observation Form	
Lesson Focus:	
How productive struggle will be implemented in the lesson:	
What I noticed about students doing the work (persistence, etc.)	What I noticed about the task

"I Spy" for Patterns With Productive Struggle

Learning walks provide a "snapshot" of what is happening in classrooms. They are not used for evaluative purposes or for individual feedback; rather, their purpose is to help teachers learn about overall instruction. Additionally, the goal is to identify areas of instructional strengths, as well as possible challenges. You are also not watching a full lesson, but are visiting for about 10 minutes. Since you are dropping in and out of classrooms, you are looking for overall patterns within a grade level, subject area, or school. You may also want to begin with looking for positive examples, in order to build trust.

	"I Spy" Pattern Notes	
	Positive Points	*Questions I Have*
Classroom One		
Classroom Two		
Classroom Three		
Patterns I Noticed		

A school in Chicago organized "I Spy" days. Teachers dropped in on classrooms for 5–10 minutes in order to identify positive examples of instruction. Teachers came back together after school with their "detective notebooks" to share what they had seen. It was an invigorating experience for teachers, who said this was the first time they had a chance to look at other classrooms. As one teacher explained, "I don't get time to visit other teachers' classes. I learned so much, and I have two new ideas I want to implement tomorrow."

Learning in Action Through Lesson Studies

Lesson studies emphasize working in small groups to plan, teach, observe, and critique a lesson. It's an excellent reflection of the principles of professional learning communities, as the goal is to systematically examine your teaching in order to become more effective.

In a lesson study, teachers work together to develop a detailed plan for a lesson. One member of the group teaches the lesson to his or her students, while other members of the group observe. Next, the group discusses their observations about the lesson and student learning.

Teachers revise the lesson based on their observations, then a second group member teaches the lesson, with other members once again observing. Then, the group meets to discuss the revised lesson. Finally, teachers talk about what the study lesson taught them and how they can apply the learning in their own classroom.

Steps in a Lesson Study

Teachers choose a lesson focus.

Teachers develop the lesson, which includes productive struggle.

One teacher teaches the lesson.

Other teachers observe the lesson, either live or on video.

Teachers discuss what they observed.

Teachers revise the lesson.

Second teacher teachers the lesson.

Other teachers observe the lesson, either live or on video.

Teacher discuss the revised lesson.

Teachers discuss what the lesson and process taught them and how they can apply the learning.

Looking at the How: Developing Consistent Expectations for the Process of Productive Struggle

It's important to have consistent expectations within a grade level, and across grade levels. Ideally, for the process of productive struggle—what productive struggle looks like and how students approach it—you want to be consistent across all teachers in your school. It may look a bit different in kindergarten and fifth grade, but there are basic expectations that should be consistent. Here's my recommended process for developing consistent expectations on the "how" of productive struggle.

Research productive struggle through books, articles, and videos.

Teachers share ideas as to what productive struggle looks like (persistence, only asking for help after trying on your own first, etc.). Take all ideas and chart them out.

Organize the ideas by patterns or categories (help seeking, using scaffolding tools, etc.).

Reword words and phrases to be student friendly.

Create a chart students can follow.

Implement the chart.

Teachers make necessary adjustments as needed.

Sample Student Chart of Productive Struggle Expectations

☺	☹
Try it yourself first.	Immediately ask the teacher for help.
If it's hard, keep trying!	Give up before you start.

Looking at Student Work: Developing Consistent Expectations for the Products of Productive Struggle

A final way to improve productive struggle is to look at authentic student work. When you examine and evaluate student work, you can clarify your own standards for work, strengthen common expectations for students, or align curriculum across classrooms.

It's important that the discussion is focused on results, not on personalities. At the beginning of the process, agree on a process for the discussion. Templates are also helpful to keep everyone on the same page.

Discuss what makes an assignment "glow" and where an assignment needs to "grow."

Grows and Glows	
What Grows and Glows?	
Grows	Glows
Overall Thoughts and Recommendations	

Looking at Student Work	
Looking in Depth at Student Work for Productive Struggle	
	Response
Did the level of the task seem appropriate (not too easy, not too hard)?	
Did the student appear to struggle with his or her work?	
Would you say the student was successful with the task?	
How did you define success for this task?	
What recommendations would you make for improvement?	

A Final Note

Collaborating with other teachers is helpful when incorporating productive struggle in the classroom. In addition to co-creating activities, learning from each other can improve your practice. Finding time to effectively collaborate is challenging, but the benefits outweigh the disadvantages.

Points to Ponder

1. Which time management tip resonated with you? How can you implement it?
2. How can you and your fellow teachers improve collaboration?
3. Which of the activities for professional learning will you try in your school?

Continue the Learning

Use the QR Code to access videos for your own use or for group professional development.

Bibliography

Amidon, J., Monroe, A., Rock, D., & Cook, C. (2020). Shame, shame, go away: Fostering productive struggle with mathematics. *Kappa Delta Pi Record*, 56(2), 64–69.

Bates, B. (2023). *Learning theories simplified: . . . and how to apply them to teaching*. London, UK: SAGE Publications Ltd.

Berger, R., Woodfin, L., & Vilen, A. (2016). *Learning that lasts*. San Francisco: Jossey Bass.

Blackburn, B. R. (2016). *Motivating struggling learners: Ten strategies for student success*. New York: Routledge.

Blackburn, B. R. (2019). *Rigor and differentiation in the classroom*. New York: Routledge.

Blackburn, B. R. (2020). *Rigor in the remote learning classroom*. New York: Routledge.

Blackburn, B. R. (2021). *Rigor in your classroom: A toolkit for teachers* (2nd ed.). New York: Routledge.

Blackburn, B. R. (2025). *Scaffolding for success*. New York: Routledge.

Blackburn, B. R. (2026a). *Rigor and assessment in the classroom*. New York: Routledge.

Blackburn, B. R. (2026b). *Rigor is not a four-letter word* (4th ed.). New York: Routledge.

Blackburn, B. R., & Armstrong, A. (2019). *Rigor in the 6-12 math and science classroom*. New York: Routledge.

Blackburn, B. R., & Armstrong, A. (2020). *Rigor in the K-5 math and science classroom*. New York: Routledge.

Blackburn, B. R., Armstrong, A., & Miles, M. (2018). Using writing to spark learning in math, science, and social studies. *ASCD Express*, 13(16). www.ascd.org/ascd-express/vol13/1316-blackburn.aspx?utm_source=ascdexpress&utm_medium=email&utm_campaign=Express%2D13%2D16

Blackburn, B. R., & Miles, M. (2019). *Rigor in the 6-12 language arts and social studies classroom*. New York: Routledge.

Blackburn, B. R., & Miles, M. (2020). *Rigor in the K-5 language arts and social studies classroom*. New York: Routledge.

Blackburn, B. R., & Witzel, B. (2018). *Rigor in the RTI/MTSS classroom*. New York: Routledge.

Blackburn, B. R., & Witzel, B. (2021). *Rigor for students with special needs* (2nd ed.). New York: Routledge.

Boryga, A. (2024, February 1). Helping young kids manage productive struggle. *Edutopia*. https://www.edutopia.org/article/helping-young-kids-manage-productive-struggle

Brown, P. C., Roediger, H. L., III, & McDaniel, M. A. (2014). *Make it stick: The science of successful learning*. The Belknap Press of Harvard University Press.

Bullmaster-Day, M. L. (2022). Key elements of productive struggle. *Waggle Blog (Renaissance Learning)*. https://blog.waggle.org/key-elements-of-productive-struggle

Bybee, R. W., Taylor, J. A., Gardner, A., Van Scotter, P., Carlson Powell, J., Westbrook, A., & Landes, N. (2006). *The BSCS 5E instructional model: Origins, effectiveness, and applications*. Colorado Springs, CO: BSCS.

Claxton, G. (2017). *The learning power approach: Teaching learners to teach themselves*. Thousand Oaks, CA: Corwin Press.

Colorado Department of Education. (n.d.). Taking action: Implementing effective mathematics teaching practices. *Colorado Dept. of Education*. https://www.cde.state.co.us/comath/mathteachingpractice7

Corwin Authors. (2024, October). Why and how to encourage productive struggle. *Corwin Connect*. https://corwin-connect.com/2024/10/corwintalks-why-and-how-to-encourage-productive-struggle/

Costa, A. L., & Kallick, B. (2008). *Learning and leading with habits of mind: 16 essential characteristics for success*. Alexandria, VA: Association for Supervision and Curriculum Development.

Costa, A. L., & Kallick, B. (2014). *Dispositions: Reframing teaching and learning*. Thousand Oaks, CA: Corwin Press.

Cowen, E. (2016). Harnessing the power of productive struggle. *Edutopia*. https://www.edutopia.org/blog/harnessing-power-of-productive-struggle-ellie-cowen

Csikszentmihalyi, M. (2009). Flow. In S. Lopez (Ed.), *The encyclopedia of positive psychology* (pp. 394–400). Chichester: Blackwell Publishing Ltd.

Dean, C. B., Hubbell, E. R., Pitler, H., Stone, B., & Marzano, R. J. (2012). *Classroom instruction that works: Research-based strategies for increasing student achievement* (2nd ed.). ASCD.

Dinkmeyer, D., & Losoncy, L. (Ed.). (1992). *The encouragement book*. New York: Simon and Schuster.

DuFour, R., DuFour, R., Eaker, R., Many, T. W., & Mattos, M. (2016). *Learning by doing: A handbook for professional learning communities at work* (3rd ed.). Bloomington, IN: Solution Tree Press.

Dweck, C. S., & Elliott, E. S. (1983). Achievement motivation. In P. Mussen & E. M. Hetherington (Eds.), *Handbook of child psychology* (pp. 643–691). New York, NY: Wiley.

Education Rickshaw. (2022, April 24). Do we want our students to struggle? *Education Rickshaw*. https://educationrickshaw.com/2022/04/24/do-we-want-our-students-to-struggle/

Elliott, E. S., & Dweck, C. S. (1988). Goals: An approach to motivation and achievement. *Journal of Personality and Social Psychology, 54*(1), 5–12.

ExploreLearning (n.d.). What is productive struggle? *ExploreLearning*. https://www.explorelearning.com/resources/insights/productive-struggle

Ferlazzo, L. (2013). *Self-driven learning: Teaching strategies for student motivation*. New York: Routledge.

The GiST. (n.d.). Foster STEM dispositions. *The GiST*. Retrieved September 3, 2025, from https://www.thegist.edu.au/educators/create-inclusive-classrooms/talk-tools-build-stem-capital/foster-stem-dispositions/?utm_source=chatgpt.com

Goodwin, B., & Rouleau, K. (2019). *The new classroom instruction that works: The best research-based strategies for increasing student achievement*. Alexandria, VA: ASCD.

Grafwallner, P. J. (2021). *Not yet . . . and that's OK: How productive struggle fosters student learning*. Bloomington, IN: Solution Tree Press.

Hall, G. E., Quinn, L. F., & Gollnick, D. M. (Eds.). (2023). *The Wiley handbook of teaching and learning*. Hoboken, NJ: John Wiley & Sons, Inc.

Hattie, J., Fisher, D., Frey, N., & Almarode, J. (2024). *The illustrated guide to visible learning*. Thousand Oaks, CA: Corwin Press.

Hess, K. (2024). *Rigor by design, not chance: Deeper thinking through actionable instruction and assessment*. Thousand Oaks, CA: Corwin Press.

Hiebert, J., & Wearne, D. (2003). Developing understanding through problem solving. In H. L. Schoen (Ed.), *Teaching mathematics through problem solving: Grades 6 – 12* (pp. 3–13). Reston, VA: National Council of Teachers of Mathematics.

HMH Staff. (2022, June 6). What is productive struggle in the classroom? *HMH*. https://www.hmhco.com/blog/what-is-productive-struggle-in-the-classroom

Johnson, A. P. (2019). *Essential learning theories: Applications to authentic teaching and learning strategies*. Lanham, MD: Rowman & Littlefield.

Kapur, M. (2016). Examining productive failure, productive success, unproductive failure, and unproductive success in learning. *Educational Psychologist, 51*(2), 289–299.

Kennedy, M. (n.d.). The key to understanding productive struggle in games. *MIND Research Institute*. https://blog.mindresearch.org/blog/the-key-to-understanding-productive-struggle-in-games-is-here

Kettler, R. J. (2012). Testing accommodations: Theory and research to inform practice. *International Journal of Disability, Development and Education, 5*, 53–66.

Khalil, I., Al-Otaibi, A., Almughyriah, S., & Almalky, M. (2025). How do students evaluate their teachers' support for productive struggle in learning mathematics? *Cogent Education*, 12(1).

Marshall, J. C. (2019). *Rise to the challenge*. Alexandria, VA: Association for Supervision and Curriculum Development.

Martin, K. (2019, November 3). The power of productive struggle. *Katie Martin*. https://katiemartin.com/2019/11/03/the-power-of-productive-struggle/

Marzano, R. J. (Ed.). (2010). *On excellence in teaching* (10th ed.). Solution Tree Press.

Marzano, R. J., Pickering, D. J., & Pollock, J. E. (2001). *Classroom instruction that works*. Alexandria, VA: Association for Supervision and Curriculum Development.

McDonnell, L. M., McLaughlin, M. J., & Morison, P. (1997). *Educating one and all: Students with disabilities and standards-based reform*. National Academy Press.

McDowell, M. (2024). *Rigor redefined: Ten teaching habits for surface, deep, and transfer learning*. Bloomington, IN: Solution Tree Press.

National Council of Teachers of Mathematics (NCTM). (2017). *Enhancing classroom practice with research behind Principles in Action*. Reston, VA: Author.

Newmann, F. M., Carmichael, D., & King, M. B. (2016). *Authentic intellectual work: Improving teaching for rigorous learning*. Thousand Oaks, CA: Corwin Press.

Nottingham, J. (2016). *Challenging learning: Theory, effective practice and lesson ideas to create optimal learning in the classroom* (2nd ed.). Routledge.

Nottingham, J. (2017). *Challenging learning through feedback: How to guide your students to be more critical, creative, and independent learners*. Corwin.

Nottingham, J. (2017). *The learning challenge*. Thousand Oaks, CA: Corwin Press.

Nottingham, J. (2024). *Teach brilliantly: Small shifts that lead to big gains in student learning*. Bloomington, IN: Solution Tree Press.

Park, J., Starett, E., Chen, Y.-C., & Jordan, M. (2024). Facilitating productive struggle in science education. *The Mathematics Enthusiast*. https://scholarworks.umt.edu/tme/vol21/iss1/7

Paurowski, M., Glassmeyer, D., Kim, J., & Id-Deen, L. (2024). Struggling as part of success: International Baccalaureate students' productive struggle is strongly correlated to mathematical achievement. *International Journal of Mathematical Education in Science and Technology*.

Ph.D. Science. (2022, December 9). How do you support students through productive struggle? *Great Minds*. https://greatminds.

org/news/phd-science/how-do-you-support-students-through-productive-struggle

Pink, D. (2009). *Drive: the surprising truth about what motivates us*. New York: Penguin Books.

Ritchhart, R. (2002). *Intellectual character: What it is, why it matters, and how to get it*. San Francisco, CA: Jossey-Bass.

Ritchhart, R. (2015). *Creating cultures of thinking: The 8 forces we must master to truly transform our schools*. San Francisco, CA: Jossey-Bass.

Ritchhart, R. (2023). *Cultures of thinking in action: 10 mindsets to transform our teaching and students' learning*. Jossey-Bass.

SanGiovanni, J., Katt, J., & Dykema, C. (2020). *Productive math struggle: A 6-point action plan for fostering perseverance*. Corwin Mathematics.

Schwartz, K. (2015, August 4). Seeing struggling math learners as 'sense makers,' not 'mistake makers'. *Mind/Shift (KQED)*. https://www.kqed.org/mindshift/40537/seeing-struggling-math-learners-as-sense-makers-not-mistake-makers

Settle, S. A., & Milich, R. (1999). Social persistence following failure in boys and girls with LD. *Journal of Learning Disabilities, 32*, 201–212.

Sibberson, F., Szymusiak, K., & Koch, L. (2008). *Beyond leveled books: Supporting early and transitional readers in grades K–5* (2nd ed.). Stenhouse Publishers.

Spencer, J. (2017). *Making learning flow*. Bloomington, IL: Solution Tree.

Sriram, R. (2020). The neuroscience behind productive struggle. *Edutopia*. https://www.edutopia.org/article/neuroscience-behind-productive-struggle/

ST Math Staff. (n.d.). The importance of productive struggle. *ST Math*. https://www.stmath.com/productive-struggle-math-rigor

STEMscopes Staff. (n.d.). 5 reasons the productive struggle belongs in STEM. *Accelerate Learning Blog*. https://blog.acceleratelearning.com/5-reasons-the-productive-struggle-belongs-in-stem

Thibodeau, T. (2024). How to harness productive struggle. *Novak Education*. https://www.novakeducation.com/blog/how-to-harness-productive-struggle

Thibodeau, T. (2024). *What is productive struggle*. https://www.novakeducation.com/blog/how-to-harness-productive-struggle

Tomlinson, C. A., & Moon, T. R. (2013). *Assessment and student success in a differentiated classroom*. Alexandria, VA: ASCD.

VanLehn, K., Burkhardt, H., Cheema, S., Kang, S., Pead, D., Schoenfeld, A., & Wetzel, J. (2019). Can an orchestration system increase collaborative, productive struggle in teaching-by-eliciting classrooms? *Interactive Learning Environments*. https://doi.org/10.1080/10494820.2019.1611657

Vygotsky, L. S. (1978). *Mind in society: The development of higher psychological processes*. Cambridge, MA: Harvard University Press.

Wagner, T. (2008). *The global achievement gap: Why even our best schools don't teach the new survival skills our children need—and what we can do about it*. New York, NY: Basic Books.

Warshauer, H. K. (2015). Strategies to support productive struggle. *Mathematics Teaching in the Middle School*, 20(7), 390–393.

Wiederhold, C. (1995). *The Q-Matrix: Cooperative Learning and Critical Thinking*. San Juan Capistrano, CA: Kagan Cooperative Learning.

Williamson, R., & Blackburn, B. (2016). *The principalship from A to Z* (2nd ed.). Routledge.

Williamson, R., & Blackburn, B. (2019). *Rigor in your school: A toolkit for leaders* (2nd ed.). New York: Routledge.

Williamson, R., & Blackburn, B. (2020). *7 strategies for improving your school*. New York: Routledge.

Williamson, R., & Blackburn, B. (2024). *Improving teacher morale and motivation*. New York: Routledge.

Witherell, J. (n.d.). Productive struggle. *Goyen Education*. https://www.goyen.io/blog/productivestruggle

Young, J. R., Bevan, D., & Sanders, M. (2024). How productive is the productive struggle? Lessons learned from a scoping review. *International Journal of Education in Mathematics, Science, and Technology*. https://doi.org/10.46328/ijemst.3364

Young, L. A. J. (2024, October 1). Thriving in the zone of productive struggle. *ASCD*. https://www.ascd.org/blogs/thriving-in-the-zone-of-productive-struggle

For Product Safety Concerns and Information please contact our EU
representative GPSR@taylorandfrancis.com
Taylor & Francis Verlag GmbH, Kaufingerstraße 24, 80331 München, Germany

www.ingramcontent.com/pod-product-compliance
Lightning Source LLC
Chambersburg PA
CBHW080732300426
44114CB00019B/2561